THE
SECRET WORLD
OF THE
SPY

THE SECRET WORLD OF THE SPY

Stories of Espionage, Deception & Discovery

WILL FOWLER

COURAGE
BOOKS

AN IMPRINT OF RUNNING PRESS
PHILADELPHIA · LONDON

PAGE 1: A handcuffed and pensive Colonel Rudolph Ivanovich Abel after arraignment on spy charges in New York. He was exchanged for the U-2 pilot Gary Powers.

PAGES 2-3: The tools of the USAF aerial reconnaissance trade — the SR-71 Blackbird and the Lockheed TR-1, which was originally known as the U-2.

BELOW RIGHT: Marguerite Zelle, better known as Mata Hari, whose oriental dancing caused a considerable stir before World War I and earned her a reputation as a femme fatale spy.

Dedication: To SL and the angels of Paradise Road

9 8 7 6 5 4 3 2 1

Digit on the right indicates the number of this printing.

Library of Congress Cataloging-in-Publication Number 93-74686

ISBN 1-56138-428-3

Printed and bound in China

Cover designed by Running Press

First published by Courage Books, an imprint of Running Press Book Publishers
125 South Twenty-second Street
Philadelphia, Pennsylvania 19103

CONTENTS

6. **INTRODUCTION**

10. **THE AGENTS**

34. **THE MISSIONS**

52. **THE MEANS**

72. **THE METHODS**

94. **THE MYTHS**

126. **INDEX**

128. **ACKNOWLEDGMENTS**

INTRODUCTION

Espionage – actions directed toward the acquisition of information through clandestine means.

This definition of espionage by the U.S. Department of Defense (DoD) and Inter-American Defense Board (IADB) shows the considerable breadth of interpretation that can be applied to the term "espionage." It can cover anything from the classic 1940s and 1950s image of the agent gaining illegal access to a government building or arms factory and using a miniature camera to photograph plans or documents, to the reconnaissance satellite high above the earth.

Strictly speaking, even soldiers in uniform on a reconnaissance patrol, or concealed in a covert observation post, are practicing a form of espionage, since they are gathering information by stealth. In China in 500 B.C. Sun Tzu Wu, whose *Art of War* is the oldest military treatise in the world, predicted almost all the permutations of espionage.

Knowledge of the enemy's dispositions can only be obtained from other men. Hence the use of spies, of whom there are five classes: local, inward, converted, doomed, and surviving spies.

When these five kinds of spy are all at work, none can discover all of the ramifications of your secret spy system. This is called "divine manipulation of the threads." It is the sovereign's most precious faculty:
Local spying – invaders employing the services of the inhabitants of a district.
Inward spies – making use of enemy officials.

Converted spies – getting hold of the enemy's spies and using them for our own purposes.
Doomed spies – doing certain things openly for purposes of deception, and allowing our own spies to know them and report them to the enemy (when captured).
Surviving spies – those who bring back news from the enemy's camp.

Sun Tzu Wu even anticipates the murky world of counterespionage and "turning" enemy operators when he goes on to write:

The enemy's spies who have come to spy on us must be sought out, tempted with bribes, led away, and comfortably housed. Thus they will become converted spies and available for our service.

Another ancient ploy which is still used is the "honey trap." This uses a glamorous woman or man, depending on the target's tastes or sex, who, following an affair, blackmails or charms information out of a civil-service employee or military officer. All these activities are part of the intelligence-gathering operation of a nation, conducted through its military and governmental agencies. Perhaps at this point it is worth looking at the NATO definition of intelligence.

The product resulting from the processing of information concerning foreign nations, hostile or potentially hostile forces or elements, or areas of actual or potential operations. The term is also applied to the activity which results in the product, and organizations engaged in such activity.

RIGHT: The tools of the trade for a World War II agent. These include a radio transmitter, listening devices, a Welrod silenced pistol, full-size and miniature cameras, a leg dagger, German and British booby trap mechanisms, pen dagger, time pencil, and a hand magneto torch. Many of these devices are still in service, except that they are smaller and made from non-magnetic materials.

This is much more helpful, but does not cover the increasing area of industrial espionage, which may be directed by commercial operators or even government agencies against the manufacturers and design teams of friendly nations. Nor does the definition fully embrace the intelligence operations directed against terrorist or subversive organizations within a country.

If this definition has only partly penetrated the murk and confusion of the world of espionage, the DoD and IADB definition of the "intelligence cycle" may shed a little more light.

The steps by which information is converted into intelligence and made available to users. There are five steps in the cycle:

a. Planning and direction – Determination of intelligence requirements, preparation of a collection plan, issuance of orders and requests to information collection agencies, and a continuous check on the productivity of collection agencies.

b. Collection – Acquisition of information and the provision of this information to processing and/or production elements.

c. Processing – Conversion of collected information into a form suitable to the production of intelligence.

d. Production – Conversion of information into intelligence through the integration,

analysis, evaluation, and interpretation of all sources of data and preparation of intelligence products in support of known or anticipated user requirements.

As these official definitions suggest, the gathering of information by covert means is only part of a wider intelligence operation. The correct briefing of the spy

ABOVE: The U-2 first flew in 1955, and remains a versatile and effective reconnaissance platform.

BELOW: A photograph taken by a U-2 of a Soviet IRBM site at Guanajay, Cuba. These pictures triggered the Cuban Missile Crisis of 1962.

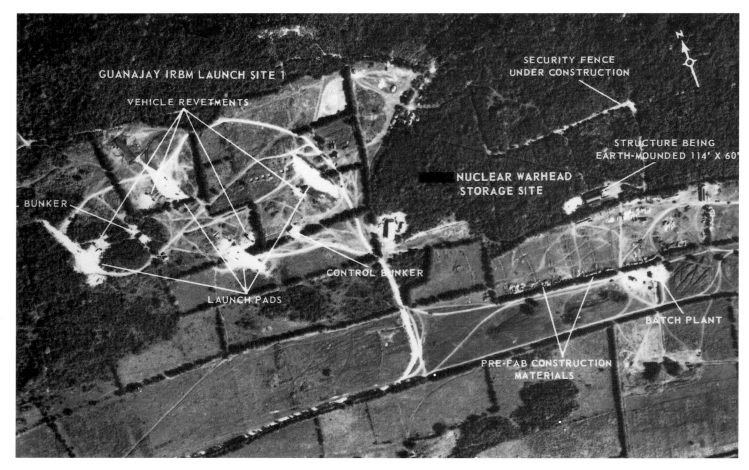

GUANAJAY IRBM LAUNCH SITE 1

VEHICLE REVETMENTS

SECURITY FENCE UNDER CONSTRUCTION

STRUCTURE BEING EARTH-MOUNDED 114' X 60'

NUCLEAR WARHEAD STORAGE SITE

BUNKER

CONTROL BUNKER

LAUNCH PADS

BATCH PLANT

PRE-FAB CONSTRUCTION MATERIALS

and the subsequent evaluation of this information helps to build up a wider picture. It is very rare that there are major intelligence "breaks." The picture is normally built up from a mass of information, sometimes apparently contradictory, sometimes repetitive, but like a jigsaw puzzle it comes together to reveal a pattern or picture. Increasingly this process uses equipment – computers, still and video photography, radio signal intercepts, and decryption. However, despite these aids, intelligence still relies on human judgment and the ability of operatives to follow up an intelligence hunch or discard a fruitless course.

Many of the information-gathering techniques developed and perfected during the Cold War are now less relevant. Satellites with cameras so sensitive that they can read a car license plate from space were fine when part of the threat was a Soviet and Warsaw Pact surprise attack through the Fulda Gap into Western Europe, but they are of less use now. Intelligence gathering has shifted back to HUMINT (human intelligence) in an attempt to understand or guess at the thoughts and plans of national leaders who, through politics or religion, have the power to destabilize areas of international importance.

As the observations of Sun Tzu Wu show, espionage is one of the oldest callings in the world. No book can adequately cover the personalities and permutations of the trade, but this volume will give the reader chapters which are "intelligence leads," with examples drawn largely from the Cold War and the uncertain times of the mid- and late-twentieth century. Chapters will cover both the men and women, the missions, the means, the methods with which they have operated, and finally the myths associated with the trade.

ABOVE: J. Edgar Hoover was the head of the Federal Bureau of Investigation for half a century. His methods at the close of his career were distinctly undemocratic, and included tapping the telephone lines of anti-Vietnam War protesters. However he kept the Bureau out of the Watergate scandal. Hoover died in 1972.

THE AGENTS

The forces that have motivated spies over the centuries are often complex and diverse. They may serve willingly, through pressure or coercion, for financial gain, out of religious or political conviction, or simply as a career intelligence operator. But whatever the motivation, the controlling power sees the agent primarily as a source of information, and as such, the asset will be classified from A to D – an A-grade source being a very highly placed politician or serviceman with access to top-secret information, and a D-grade an unreliable or minor source. The information is in turn rated from 1 to 10, and by linking this alphanumerical coding, a simple classification is produced. For example, if a B-grade source provides information which is reckoned to be rather questionable, and therefore rated 3, the information is B3. The DoD and IADB definition of a source is fairly comprehensive.

(1) A person, thing, or activity from which intelligence information is obtained; (2) in clandestine activities, a person (agent), normally a foreign national, in the employ of an intelligence agency for intelligence purposes; (3) in interrogation activities, any person who furnishes intelligence information, either with or without the knowledge that the information is being used for intelligence purposes. In this context, a controlled source is in the employment or under the control of the intelligence agency and knows that the information is to be used for such purposes. An uncontrolled source is a voluntary contributor of information who may not know that the information is to be used for intelligence purposes.

Ironically, an uncontrolled source may be of greater value than an elaborately recruited or trained source. Sometimes known as a "defector in place," they may be disenchanted with their government or country, or merely their employer, and if they leave or defect, there is immediate value in their debriefing. Though foreign intelligence operators may be able to give a guide to the workings of their espionage organizations and identify hostile agents at work in the host country, who are often apparently humble engineers and technicians, diplomats may have greater intelligence value for the insights they give into their country. Donald "Jamie" Jameson, who was a senior officer in the CIA, commented at a conference in 1991: "Most really good spies are walk-ins. . . . By and large, our best agents were the agents who recruited themselves, and who finally made contact and produced their information." He cited Colonel Oleg Penkovsky and Colonel Pyotr Popov – the former gave information to the British, and the latter to the Americans.

One bizarre uncontrolled source for the U.S.S.R. was Royal Navy Sublieutenant David Bingham, a young and promising naval officer who had risen from the ranks, graduating as an officer from the naval training establishment at Dartmouth at the top of his class, and so winning the "Sword of Honor." His wife, who came from a humble background, ran up considerable gambling and domestic

RIGHT: Emil Julius Klaus Fuchs, the German-born nuclear physicist who spied for the Soviet Union out of principle. He provided the U.S.S.R. with details of the development of the atomic bombs used against Japan. He was sentenced to 14 years in jail, served nine, and then went to East Germany. After confessing to spying he hoped that he could remain in Britain, his home by adoption, and continue as head of the theoretical physics division of the Atomic Energy Establishment at Harwell.

debts attempting to emulate what she took to be the lifestyle of an officer's wife. In 1969, saddled with huge debts, Maureen Bingham traveled up to London and went to the Soviet Embassy, where she said that her husband would provide top-secret naval intelligence for cash.

The KGB paid out a four-figure sum; the Binghams settled their debts, and in turn the Soviet Union received very useful information. The intelligence concerned torpedo trials on HMS *Rothsay*, and antisubmarine technologies, including the U.S. nuclear depthcharge that had been supplied to the Royal Navy. Bingham's incompetent spying went undetected, despite the importance of the information passed on, and he was arrested only after he had confessed to his ship's first officer. Tried and found

guilty, Bingham was sentenced to 21 years, though after seven he was released on parole. He divorced his wife, and after remarrying found work with the probation service in 1982, supervising young offenders doing community work.

The danger with recruiting and running a controlled source is that he or she may be a "plant" by the hostile intelligence service. A potential source that has been approached by an intelligence operator may report this to his government's counterespionage service. This service may simply say "don't talk," or they may decide to use the source to feed false or misleading information, while finding out what the hostile service wants to know – its "information requirement."

ABOVE: Codes, notebooks, and instructions used by Oleg Penkovsky and shown at his trial. Penkovsky was executed for treason.

The core requirement in recruiting a man or woman for a career in intelligence work with a government agency, is to ensure that they are reliable and will not disclose, either by accident or under duress, information about their work or the operations they are involved in. At a very early stage the recruit will be interviewed and their background assessed – language or communication skills are obviously attractive, as is a knowledge of the world – both social and geographical. The agents may find themselves operating in an overseas embassy with a cover or alias as a commercial or press attaché, and so they will need to be able to mix at social and business functions and be convincing.

The ability to be a social chameleon means that a very striking man or woman may be at a disadvantage. The "gray man" who blends unnoticed into a crowd can be posted to different embassies around the world without attracting attention, and can attend functions or meetings without being noticed. The role of army, navy, or air defense attaché at an overseas embassy is normally held by an officer who has both intelligence training and good linguistic skills. The men in this position have some difficulty remaining "gray," but can still develop uncontrolled sources in the defense and media community.

Uncontrolled sources which proved valuable to the KGB and other Warsaw Pact agencies, but which almost overwhelmed them by their volume, were publicly available TV and radio programs, as well as books and articles in

LEFT: Greville Maynard Wynne stands trial in Moscow in May 1963. Wynne was sentenced to eight years, but was exchanged for Gordon Lonsdale after a very tough year in jail.

BELOW: Sublieutenant David Bingham receives the Sword of Honor as top student at the Royal Naval College at Dartmouth. His wife persuaded him to spy for the Soviets to cover her debts. He was sentenced to 21 years, served seven, divorced his wife, remarried, and now works in the probation service with young offenders.

magazines and newspapers. Though some of the information in autobiographies might be dated, it still gives an idea about operating techniques, targets, and priorities. Peter Wright, a former Assistant Director of British Military Intelligence Department Five, better known as MI5, which deals with counterespionage and internal subversion in the United Kingdom, wrote an autobiography in 1988 called *Spycatcher* to highlight the threat of Soviet penetration of British society and the security services. The British government attempted to suppress the book, but legal actions only served to give it greater publicity, and with it the shadowy world of MI5 in the

early 1970s. When the book was published, Peter Wright was living in Australia and so was not obliged to submit his manuscript for British approval to ensure he had not breached the U.K.'s Official Secrets Act and "endangered" national security. If he had, it might have been scrutinized by "Britain's oldest spy," Lt. Col. Edward Boxhall.

Boxhall had served in intelligence in World War I, during the 1920s and 1930s, and in the Special Operations Executive (SOE) in World War II. When, in 1979, a British magazine published a photograph taken in the 1920s of British intelligence officers, including Boxhall in uniform with Sydney Reilly, who was

RIGHT: Peter Wright, the retired senior MI5 officer who wrote *Spycatcher*, outside the Australian Supreme Court in Sydney at the hearing in which the British government attempted to get the book banned. He remained a droll, well-informed participant in the hearings, which eventually went against the British government.

ABOVE: Captain Sydney Reilly MC, the "Ace of Spies," who gave the British government valuable insights into the nascent Soviet Union. A Russian Jew, he claimed as an alias that his father was an Irish sea captain. Other names that Reilly went by included Comrade Relisky, Georg Bergmann, and Monsieur Massimo. The head of MI1, Sir William Wiseman, described him as "a sinister man who I could never bring myself wholly to trust."

damaging was known or suspected. In 1947 there were moves to introduce "positive vetting," which involved active investigation of an individual's past. Following the scandals of Klaus Fuchs (the atomic scientist), and Burgess and Maclean (the British traitors who penetrated the upper echelons of the Establishment), the United States put pressure on the British, with whom they shared defense secrets, to make positive vetting mandatory.

The potential recruit may be interviewed using a polygraph lie detector – in intelligence jargon this is known as being "boxed" or "fluttered," since the equipment shows the subject's respiratory and pulse rates which rise if they supply false information. It is a pretty reliable way of checking, but there have been instances of agents who have – with preparation and practice, and a fair idea of the questions they are likely to receive – remained calm and bluffed their way through a lie-detector test. Questions under a polygraph can be stressful even if the subject has no guilty secrets, but the equipment is normally checked at the beginning by asking the subject an embarrassing question about his or her personal or sex life which they are likely to want to evade or conceal.

It has been reported that KGB agents were trained to "block" physical reactions when being questioned under a polygraph. In his fascinating biography of John Vann who headed the USAID program in Vietnam, Neil Sheehan described how Vann "beat" the polygraph. Vann had had an affair with a young girl while he was in the U.S. Army and knew that he would be questioned by investigators.

Vann obtained tranquilizers and drugs to lower blood pressure. He bought a physician's instrument for measuring blood pressure. He timed the rate of his pulse beats with his watch. He drew up lists of questions about his affair with the girl. He arranged the questions in the sequence he believed a polygraph operator would follow. He put himself through mock investigations, changing the questions and sequences from one interrogation to another so that he would not be surprised. He interrogated himself with and without the various medications. He took notes on his bodily reactions. He finally decided that he seemed best able to slow down his reactions, and not run the risk of appearing to have drugged himself, simply by staying awake for 48 hours and answering the questions in a confident manner.

known as the "Ace of Spies," there was an official complaint that Boxhall's cover had been "blown." When he died at the age of 86 in 1984, he was said to be still in active service, vetting manuscripts for books by retired officers of the British security services.

Assuming that a would-be recruit to the intelligence services has crossed the first hurdle, he or she will undergo rigorous vetting or screening, involving in-depth interviews with the person and their friends or associates. In the United Kingdom during World War II, security personnel went through "negative vetting," which in effect established that they were fit for the job if nothing

The purpose behind vetting is to establish whether the potential recruit has any areas of weakness that might be exploited by a hostile organization to blackmail or pressurize the agent in some way. The priorities of vetting can be summarized under the heading MICE – Money, Ideology, Compromise, and Ego – all of which are areas that can be exploited either in recruiting agents or penetrating a hostile intelligence network. Vetting also extends to any personnel who have access to secret or confidential material that may be targeted by hostile agencies. It is worth digressing here to examine the DoD definitions of the three security classifications, since this information is the target for hostile intelligence agents.

a. Top Secret – National security information or material which requires the highest degree of protection and the unauthorized disclosure of which could reasonably be expected to cause exceptionally grave damage to the national security. Examples of "exceptionally grave damage" include armed hostilities against the United States or its allies; disruption of foreign relations vitally affecting the national security; the compromise of vital national defense plans or complex cryptologic and communications intelligence systems; the revelation of sensitive intelli-

ABOVE: Tony Benn, left-wing former Labour party cabinet minister, formerly known as Sir Anthony Wedgwood Benn, reads extracts from Peter Wright's book *Spycatcher* in Hyde Park on August 2, 1987, as part of the Campaign for Press and Broadcasting Freedom.

gence operations; and the disclosure of scientific or technological developments vital to national security.

b. Secret – National security information or material which requires a substantial degree of protection and the unauthorized disclosure of which could reasonably be expected to cause serious damage to the national security. Examples of "serious damage" include disruption of foreign relations significantly affecting the national security; significant impairment of a program or policy directly related to the national security; revelation of significant military plans or intelligence operations; and compromise of significant scientific or technological developments relating to national security.

c. Confidential – National security information or material which requires protection and the unauthorized disclosure of which could reasonably be expected to cause damage to the national security.

The British National Security Classifications similarly include "top secret," "secret," and "confidential," but there is also the additional category of "restricted," which refers to information whose disclosure would be "undesirable."

During World War II, the Allies were able to intercept and decode signals sent by the German Enigma encryption machine. This ability to read the enemy's secret communications was so sensitive a secret, that it received a new classifica-

LEFT: John Vassall, a clerk working in the office of the British naval attaché in Moscow, was a homosexual who was compromised in 1955 by the KGB and blackmailed and bribed into spying. At a press conference launching his autobiography in 1972, he commented that by the 1970s homosexuality no longer carried any stigma, and he would not now have been vulnerable to blackmail. He was sentenced to 18 years in prison in 1962 but was released on parole in 1973.

The newspaper reproduced here bears its own text, part of which reads:

'MOSCOW BLACKMAIL AFTER DRINKS'

Secrets Case Story Of A Pink Chalk Circle On A Tree In Duchess Of Bedford Walk And Phone Call To 'Miss Mary'

LEFT: How the British public learned about Vassall's operations on October 9, 1962. The newspaper article lists the London Underground stations where Vassall met contacts. Though the chalk marks on trees were a standard technique for fixing assignations, the Soviets took a risk meeting in person — later techniques used the "dead-letter box." Some of the intelligence that Vassall passed is believed to have assisted the Soviet Navy in the design of helicopter carriers *Moskva* and *Leningrad*, which are similar to HMS *Invincible*, the Royal Navy's first helicopter carrier.

tion level — it was "Ultra Secret." Ultra has remained the common name for this highly sophisticated SIGINT (signals intelligence) operation since World War II.

Usually, even routine confidential material is protected, since it may be used in a roundabout way to gain access to secret, and even top-secret, information. While classified information may be discovered by mechanical or electronic means, it may also be revealed through simple human weakness, which is why vetting is so important. Human weakness is one way in which a spy can be recruited. One of the vulnerable areas is sex. The threat to reveal secret homosexuality may be used as a blackmail technique. The provision of discreet high-class prostitutes for men who, through age or circumstance, have little opportunity to enjoy a sex life, can be exploited either for blackmail or regulated as a way of paying for information — the women themselves may even be asked to find out information.

In 1955 John Vassall, a clerk working in the office of the British naval attaché in Moscow, was photographed drunk at a party in compromising homosexual postures. Blackmail and payments kept him

in the service of the KGB until he was arrested in 1962. Today, however, changing social attitudes have removed some of the stigma associated with extramarital heterosexual liaisons or homosexual activities. Interestingly, Admiral Bobby Inman, who at 46 was the youngest-ever director of the U.S. National Security Agency (NSA), confronted the problem of the homosexuality of a member of his staff in the 1970s, by ensuring that the man inform his family and write an undertaking that he would not allow his sexual leanings to be used as a blackmail weapon. The man kept his job.

The NSA was particularly sensitive to the problem of homosexuals in its service because two gay analysts, Bernon Mitchell and William Martin, had defected to Moscow in 1960 and appeared at a press conference in Moscow denouncing the United States. They brought with them information about the U-2 high-altitude reconnaissance aircraft and revealed details of Government Communications Headquarters (GCHQ), the NSA's sister organization in the United Kingdom.

The British spy, Geoffrey Prime, who worked in the GCHQ at Cheltenham, supplied highly classified information to the KGB out of misguided political conviction and the sense of excitement that espionage engendered. However, it was his misguided sexual tastes that led to his arrest. An inadequate loner who, though married twice, clearly welcomed the sense of importance and value that his contacts with Soviet intelligence gave him, he was told that he held the rank of colonel in the KGB and that if he needed to defect he would be paid and accommodated according to his rank in the U.S.S.R.

Prime was also a pedophiliac who was obsessed with young girls, and although arrested by the police in 1981 following an attack on a girl, it was only as a result of the intervention of his wife that his spying career came to light. He had confessed it to her after a visit by the police. For his Soviet masters, Prime had ceased to be of real interest since he had resigned from GCHQ. He was tried and found guilty at the Old Bailey (the U.K.'s highest criminal court) and sentenced to 38 years in prison – 35 for spying and three for sexual offenses.

At the height of the Cold War, in June 1956, a semifreelance KGB operation headed by Yuri Krotkov attempted to use sexual favors to blackmail Maurice

ABOVE: William H. Martin (left) and Bernon F. Mitchell, the former a cryptologist and the latter an officer in the U.S. Navy, who defected to the U.S.S.R. from the U.S.A. in 1960. Though both men worked for the highly secret National Security Agency and had been vetted, they felt under pressure due to a purge of 26 homosexuals at the NSA who were fired on the grounds of "indications of sexual deviation." They gave the KGB details of the links between the NSA and Government Communications Headquarters (GCHQ) in Cheltenham, England. After several years in the U.S.S.R., Mitchell became disillusioned with life there, particularly since Martin had married a Soviet, but was told that he could not return to the U.S.A. since he had been stripped of his American citizenship.

Dejean, the French ambassador in Moscow. The plot, code-named Operation Seduction, involved the use of "swallows" – women who were prepared to offer sexual favors for personal advancement, who entrapped the ambassador and his air attaché. An unsuccessful attempt was even made to entangle the ambassador's wife, Marie-Claire. The ambassador was compromised with two different women, and in one near-comic scene, the "husband" of the beautiful actress Larissa Kronberg-Sobolevskaya returned to find his "wife" in bed with the ambassador.

"It's my husband!" screamed the actress in her best theatrical voice. The "husband," dressed in boots and outdoor clothes fresh from his "geological expedition to Siberia," then beat the ambassador. Only after Larissa had pleaded for

ABOVE: A partial copy of the telegram sent by Mitchell to his father when the U.S. Navy officer defected. Mitchell and Martin may have provided the Soviet Union with the information that enabled them to shoot down the U-2 flown by Gary Powers in May 1960.

THE WIFE: I forgive him, she says after Old Bailey trial

THE SPY: Most important Russian agent, say Americans

LEFT: Geoffrey Prime, who after service with the RAF entered GCHQ at Cheltenham, was a Russian linguist with an important job at the communications center. He passed to the Soviet Union details of the signals intelligence collected by the U.S. Rhyolite and Argus intelligence satellites. The KGB could cross-check this with information supplied by Boyce and Daulton Lee in California. In November 1982 Prime was sentenced to 38 years in jail, 35 for spying and only three for sexual offenses against young girls.

the dashing 56-year-old Frenchman was the ambassador allowed to escape. Farce turned to tragedy when the air attaché Colonel Louis Guibaud, confronted with compromising photographs by the KGB, shot himself rather than betray his country. This suicide had a profound effect on Krotkov, who subsequently defected to the United Kingdom during an official visit in 1963. When, to its chagrin, French intelligence was informed by its British counterpart about the Soviet operation, President Charles de Gaulle summoned Ambassador Dejean and uttered the pithy comment, "Eh bien, Dejean, on couche," which roughly translates as "OK, Dejean, you sleep around."

Five years later, the KGB attempted to entrap Sir Geoffrey Harrison, the British ambassador to Moscow. An attractive maid named Galya was placed in the embassy and, after they had made love in

the embassy laundry, the KGB confronted the ambassador. He refused to cooperate and when he was questioned by an MI5 counterespionage officer, the real concern was not his affair, but the fact that the photographs had been taken inside the embassy, which was meant to be a secure building. However, it later emerged that he had a real affection for the Soviet maid and met her in Leningrad at her "brother's" apartment, which was conveniently close to his hotel.

Sexual entrapment need not be as overt and clumsy as these KGB operations. In the late 1970s Rhona Ritchie, First Secretary in the British Embassy in Tel Aviv, became a very good friend of Rafaat el-Ansary, who worked in the recently established Egyptian Embassy. The Israeli press subsequently gleefully called him "the Don Juan of the Nile," but for a time the young Egyptian in-

ABOVE: The French ambassador in Moscow, Maurice Dejean, seen here presenting his credentials to M. Voroshilov at the Kremlin in 1953, was targeted for sexual blackmail by the KGB. Yuri Krotkov, who used attractive girls known as "swallows" to seduce diplomats and businessmen in Moscow, directed the operation against the French and even attempted to compromise the ambassador's wife — unlike her husband, she was made of sterner stuff.

telligence officer and the attractive and intelligent Scot enjoyed a public and entirely innocent affair. It was only after Ritchie showed el-Ansary telegrams, which included details of a multinational force to police the peace in Sinai, that she got into trouble.

At her trial at the Old Bailey, her defense counsel emphasized that she was not a spy, but rather someone who was guilty of an error of judgment and indiscretion. This incident highlighted the problems diplomats face when deciding what they can reveal off the record to other diplomats, or indeed even the press. The British Embassy, which should have been more alert, was unaware that this leak had taken place, and it was only after Mossad, the Israeli intelligence service, informed it that it acted. Ritchie received a nine-month suspended sentence and resigned from the Diplomatic Service – el-Ansary was promoted by the Egyptians and posted to Vienna.

Other vulnerable areas which may lead an individual to betray their country, are debt and feelings of guilt associated with financial mismanagement. Debt walks hand in hand with greed, and an agent may be able to recruit a foreign asset by offering to pay off their debts. The United States, which had shared many secrets with GCHQ in England was understandably unhappy at the revelations following the arrest of Prime, and insisted that polygraph tests be taken by staff at the monitoring station. However, the United States was soon to be shocked by a similar spy scandal, which former KGB sources have since said gave them even more information than Prime.

The Walker spy ring was motivated by straightforward greed. On May 20, 1984, the FBI, acting on a tip-off from his wife, arrested John Anthony Walker, a former member of the U.S. Navy. The FBI had followed Walker as he drove into the countryside to dump some "trash," which was in fact a "dead-letter box" (somewhere where agents can leave information for their masters), and the bag was filled with classified documents which were due to be collected by a Soviet agent. Following questioning, the FBI arrested Walker's son, Seaman Michael Lance Walker; Walker's older brother, retired Lt. Commander Arthur James Walker; and Jerry Alfred Whitworth, another former U.S. Navy man.

It emerged that Walker and Whitworth had provided the Soviet Union with daily copies of the "key cards" which

were used to program KW-7 cryptographic equipment. These "key cards" specified alpha-numeric codes for one-time use only, which were designed to ensure security by ruling out the possibility of code-breaking. The Walkers even supplied design manuals which allowed the KGB to construct a working replica of the machine. With this, the Soviet agencies

ABOVE: Former U.S. Navy radio technician Jerry Whitworth, during his trial in March 1986 as part of the Walker spy ring, leaves the Federal Building in San Francisco. He was charged with espionage and tax fraud.

LEFT: An FBI agent, right, identifies himself to Seaman Michael Lance Walker, at the moment of his arrest at the Andrews Air Force Base on May 25, 1985. The agent at the center carries a mailbag full of confiscated documents.

BELOW: The leader of the Walker spy ring, John Walker, leaves the detention center at Rochville *en route* for the U.S. District Court in Baltimore on October 10, 1985. Unlike earlier spy rings, the Walkers were motivated by greed rather than political conviction or blackmail pressure.

were able to decrypt more than one million classified messages.

However, the replica machine finally ceased functioning and, despite hard work by Jerry Whitworth, the KGB were unable to rectify this fault. Among the areas in which the Walker spy ring damaged the U.S. Navy were submarine and antisubmarine operations. The motive that drove the Walker ring was not political conviction or sexual guilt, but greed: the men were paid for their work by the U.S.S.R. Interestingly, debt, like many aspects of sexuality, has become less of a taboo subject in the late 1980s and early 1990s and so the scope for blackmail has diminished. But greed will always be a motive for treason, and just as the Cold War spy scandals were thought to be a thing of the past, another damaging scandal rocked the CIA.

A former section-chief of the CIA's Soviet counterintelligence operation, Aldrich Hazen Ames, was accused of feeding top-secret information, first to the Soviets and then to the Russians, in exchange for $1.5 million. Ames was said to have been "fingered" by a KGB double agent, and after a two-year investigation into his home computer files and bank records, Ames and his Colombian-born wife Maria were finally arrested in February 1994. Ames was alleged to have passed on information concerning classified CIA operations, human assets, and

personnel for nine years. Ames may even have been responsible for the alarming number of U.S. agents uncovered in the U.S.S.R. in the mid-1980s.

Cravings for drink or drugs can be exploited, too, either by threats to expose the vice, or by pandering to it. Such was the case with Frank Bossard, who had been commissioned from the ranks in the Royal Air Force during World War II, and subsequently found work in the 1960s with the Air Ministry department specializing in guided-missile research. He had become a heavy drinker, and it was in a bar that he was first approached by the KGB. Beside being a drinker, Bossard needed money, and so a deal was

LEFT: After serving their time in jail, Harry Houghton kisses Ethel "Bunty" Gee as they meet, for the first time since their arrest, in the New Forest in England on May 13, 1970. They were part of the Portland spy ring which passed naval intelligence from the Underwater Weapons Establishment to the Soviet spy Gordon Lonsdale, who was in reality Konon Trofimovich Molodi. Molodi/Lonsdale was exchanged for Greville Wynne in Berlin.

struck – cash for missile information. He was arrested in the Ivanhoe Hotel, Bloomsbury, London, in 1965, where he was photographing secret material. He wisely kept his espionage equipment in the checkroom at Waterloo station and photographed the classified documents in his lunch hour. He was found guilty in May 1965 and sentenced to 21 years in prison.

A pub in Dorset, England, was the meeting place for a retired Royal Navy petty officer, Harry Houghton, and Ethel "Bunty" Gee, who worked at the Underwater Weapons Establishment at Portland. Houghton was already working for the Soviets, with Gordon Lonsdale as his contact. Ethel Gee became part of the "Portland spy ring," providing information on weapons developments. Lonsdale, Gee, and Houghton were caught handing over Admiralty files and film at the Old Vic theater in London in 1962.

Professor Hugh Hambleton, a man with dual Canadian and British nationality, was recruited in 1947 by Vladimir Bourdine, the Soviet cultural attaché, at an Ottawa cocktail party. He was a highly public figure who enjoyed access to sensitive NATO material and gave insights into the Canadian political scene. His vice was arrogance and flattery – he thought he was too important to be prosecuted and said "he identified not so much with the KGB as 'with the officer class'." Christopher Dobson and Ronald Payne described him, in their book *The Dictionary of Espionage*, as "a bit of an international elitist, a gossip columnist of a spy." Denounced by a double agent, Hambleton avoided arrest and prosecution by the Canadians, but when stopping over in London on a trip to Spain he was arrested, prosecuted, found guilty, and sent to prison for 10 years.

At the opposite extreme from Professor Hambleton, but no less damaging to the West, was Sergeant Robert Johnson; a man with a drink problem, no future, and plenty of grudges. He thought that if he defected to the East in 1952 he might become a radio star for the Soviets. They had other plans, however, and their patience paid off, for Johnson was eventually posted to the Armed Forces Courier Station at Orly airport near Paris.

This was a very secure staging post for communications between the U.S. forces in Europe and the Pentagon. Through Johnson the KGB were able to gain access on Saturday nights when Johnson was on duty and few other personnel were around. These operations continued until April 1963. The quality of the material was so high that it was shown to the Soviet Communist party chairman Nikita Khrushchev. Johnson was posted back to the United States, and after he had gone absent without leave and taken a drunken bus ride to Las Vegas, his Austrian wife was interviewed by the FBI and the espionage story emerged. He was tried and sentenced in July 1965 to 25 years in prison. In 1971 his son, returning from service in Vietnam, visited his 52-year-old father in prison and stabbed him to death.

ABOVE: Army sergeant Robert Lee Johnson, a former Pentagon courier, who gave Soviet intelligence access to secure signals passing through Orly airport near Paris. The information was so sensitive that it was shown to Nikita Khrushchev. Johnson was sentenced to 25 years in prison. While in jail in 1971 he was visited by his son (who had served in Vietnam) who stabbed him to death.

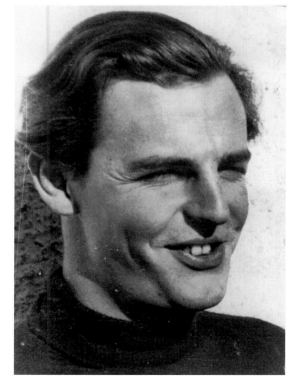

ABOVE: Exhibiting the charm that was his hallmark, Harold "Kim" Philby is pictured at a press conference at his mother's home in 1955, after he had been cleared of being the "Third Man" who had tipped off defectors Burgess and Maclean.

FAR LEFT: Guy Burgess while he was a student at Cambridge. As a member of the Apostles, a left-wing student group, he was cultivated by Soviet recruiters.

LEFT: Donald Maclean, when he was still a "beautiful man" in the eyes of Melinda his wife. She later left him in favor of Kim Philby after following him to the Soviet Union.

Heavy drinking or drug use can be an obvious vice which colleagues or security staff can become aware of. Far harder to detect are the individuals who spy out of political conviction. They do not amass large bank accounts or adopt unusual life-styles, and they may be placed as "sleepers" to be activated when their masters require information. In the late-twentieth century, political or nationalist motivation now drives the members of terrorist cells, who live frugally and can blend into society and are therefore hard to detect and arrest. Many of the wartime and immediate postwar Soviet spies had become Communists out of conviction in the 1930s, when they feared the rise of Fascism and saw the U.S.S.R. as the only power that was opposing Nazi Germany and Fascist Italy. Some of the postwar spies were idealists who thought the world would be more secure if the secrets of atomic weapons were shared between East and West.

Probably the most damaging of the wartime and postwar spy circles which was motivated principally by politics, was the group of Cambridge undergraduates who in the 1930s had formed themselves into a society known as "The Apostles." It was initially thought to consist of Harold "Kim" Philby, Guy Burgess and Donald Maclean, since all these men defected to the U.S.S.R. in the 1950s. There was much talk of a "fourth man" who had been part of the circle, but it was not until Andrew Boyle's book *The Climate of Treason* appeared in 1979 that the name of Sir Anthony Blunt became public. Blunt, a noted art historian, had been Surveyor of the Queen's Paintings until he retired. In order to avoid the embarrassment of a public trial, he was merely interrogated and stripped of his knighthood. He did not go to prison, and died at the age of 76.

What makes this operation so significant is that the Soviet Union recruited

BELOW: Mrs. Maclean with daughter Melinda after leaving her husband, whose drinking, sexual habits, and anti-American attitudes made him intolerable. She finally returned to the United States. When he died, a lonely alcoholic, he left Melinda £5000 Sterling in a frozen bank account in London.

74, FROBISHER RD.

TUESDAY,
JULY 2, 1963
THREEPENCE
No. 14716 •

Daily Herald

The world this morning

● Faint but pursuing, Britain's security services catch up, after 12 years, with the "third man" in the Burgess and Maclean affair. At least they don't actually catch up with him — they don't know where he is — but they give him a name. He is vanished journalist and ex-Foreign Office official Harold Philby. He tipped off Burgess that it was time to get out and Burgess passed the word to Maclean.

Although Philby had to resign from the Foreign Officer for Communist associations, he was cleared by Mr. Macmillan of any tip-off guilt. And Colonel Lipton, M P, who accused Philby, had to eat his words. Now Colonel Lipton wants Mr. Macmillan to eat *his* words.

Unanswered question: Who told Philby it was time to skip? (this page and P.3; Voice of the Herald, P.6).

British Cuba?

British Guiana—the remote colony which is the centre of a cold war clash and has all the makings of another Cuba *(P.2 Comment).*

Tangled

Behind this month's Moscow talks on a nuclear test ban there is a long, tangled story of frustration *(The Herald Explains, P.4).*

Joking apart

And please don't imagine there is anything funny about a comedian playing golf *(Henry Fielding, P.6).*

Plain silly

Hereditary right to drive a car without an L-test? Hereditary right to sing at Covent Garden without a voice? *Silly? No sillier than the House of Lords (Malcolm Muggeridge, P.6).*

What a laugh

A funny thing happened to Oswald Houghton as he was crossing a railway line. He was run over by an engine. *And it only made him laugh (P.7).*

Unfashionable

The revolt of the Paris midinettes. They find that fashion is not so paying as shorthand *(Off the Cuff, P.8).*

Enthusiast

New boss of I T A—Lord Hill of Luton — admits to being an enthusiastic viewer. *Of which Channel is not revealed (P.9).*

Hated exam

Britain's most hated exam, the 11-plus, has another very welcome nail knocked in its coffin *(P.9).*

Sport

Top seed Roy Emerson crashes at Wimbledon — and the man who beat him, 24-year-old German Wilhelm Bungert, had already booked his plane home! *(back page).*

Unfair, they say

The last-minute withdrawal of Relko from the Irish Derby last Saturday is still having repercussions. Each-way backers of other horses are complaining that the reduced odds have cut their winnings unfairly *(P.11).*

Chanticleer

Clean away—the man who warned Burgess and Maclean

MEN HE AIDED—BURGESS AND MACLEAN

Philby—tipped off Burgess and Maclean

WAS THIRD MAN PHILBY TIPPED OFF?

By W. N. EWER

HAROLD (KIM) PHILBY, journalist and ex-diplomat, was revealed yesterday as the "third man" who helped Guy Burgess and Donald Maclean to flee Britain 12 years ago.

Now the big security question is: Why did Philby himself suddenly vanish in January from his home in Beirut, in the Lebanon? Was he tipped off by a *fourth* man that the security services were after him?

Mr. Edward Heath, the Lord Privy Seal, told the House of Commons that Philby is now probably behind the Iron Curtain.

And it has at last been officially stated that Philby—a former First Secretary at the British Embassy in Washington — was working for the Russians when he was still a Foreign Office man.

It was Philby, then a First Secretary at the British Embassy in Washington, who tipped off diplomats Burgess and Maclean that they were under suspicion — and so enabled them to make their getaway to Russia, where they are today.

Now history repeats itself. Like Burgess and Maclean, 51-year-old Philby bolted when the net was beginning to close.

Philby resigned from the Foreign Service in July, 1951—soon after the pair vanished. He was asked to do so.

Since resigning he has worked as a journalist. At the time of his disappearance in January he was Middle East correspondent for The Observer.

Better late than never, the security services gathered evidence to justify an accusation that Philby had worked as a Soviet agent while he was a British diplomat.

EVIDENCE

In the Commons yesterday Mr. Heath said the security services were now aware of Philby's Soviet connection "apparently as a result of an admission by Mr. Philby himself."

He qualified that later by saying "there was, *in part*, the admission of Mr. Philby himself."

Did somebody, knowing that security were assembling the evidence, challenge Philby—and by doing so warn him?

If so, who was it, and by whose authority was this done?

Or was this admission made—and reported to security—*after* Philby's disappearance?

If so, it was not the cause of the disappearance, and Philby must have had some other warning.

FRANCIS MOIR writes: Mr. Heath told the House that the Foreign Office had seen letters sent "from behind the Iron Curtain" by Philby to his wife, who is now in Britain.

Last night a Foreign Office spokesman told me: "We became aware of Philby's treachery shortly before his disappearance."

Could Britain have stopped his flight from the Lebanon?

"For the last seven years he has been living outside British legal jurisdiction," Mr. Heath told the House.

MAN WHO WENT TO DINNER—PAGE 3

MRS. PHILBY
Received letters

Man who was cleared by Macmillan

By HAROLD HUTCHINSON
Herald Political Correspondent

MR. MACMILLAN will be challenged in the House of Commons today to justify statements he made as Foreign Secretary eight years ago exonerating Harold Philby as the "third man" in the Burgess and Maclean case.

The challenge will be made by Colonel Marcus Lipton, Labour MP for Brixton.

In October, 1955, Colonel Lipton named Philby as the Foreign Office official who tipped off Burgess and Maclean so that they were able to escape to Moscow before arrest.

Another Labour M P, Colonel George Wigg, gave notice last night that he will try to raise the whole question of the accuracy of a speech which Mr. Macmillan made in a debate on the Burgess and Maclean case in November, 1955.

Withdrew

After that debate Colonel Lipton, as a result of Mr. Macmillan's speech, and in fairness to Mr. Philby, unreservedly withdrew allegations he made—allegations which are now officially admitted to be true.

Colonel Lipton had asked Sir Anthony Eden, then Prime Minister, whether he had made up his mind "to cover up the judicious third man activities of Mr. Harold Philby."

The House debated the Burgess and Maclean disappearance on November 7, 1955. Mr. Macmillan, then Foreign Secretary, spoke of the possibility that Burgess and Maclean had been tipped off that the security net was closing in on them.

Resigned

"In this connection," said Mr. Macmillan, "the name of one man has been mentioned in the House but not outside.

"He is Mr. H. A. R. Philby, who was temporary First Secretary at the British Embassy in Washington from October, 1949, to June, 1951, and had been privy to much of the investigation (into Burgess and Maclean's suspected espionage activities)."

Philby and Burgess had been friends from their undergraduate days at Cambridge. Philby had Communist associates during and after university.

Mr. Macmillan said that in view of the circumstances" Philby was asked in July, 1951, to resign from the Foreign Service.

He added: "Since that date he has been the subject of close investigation. No evidence has been found showing that he was responsible for warning Burgess or Maclean."

Conscientious

"While in the Government service he carried out his duties ably and conscientiously.

"I have no reason to conclude," added Mr. Macmillan, "that Mr. Philby has at any time betrayed the interest of this country or to identify him with the so-called third man if indeed there was one."

Last night Colonel Lipton and Colonel Wigg said that "although bit by bit the truth is beginning to emerge we are not satisfied that the whole truth has been stated."

Many M Ps believe the decision to make the announcement yesterday was forced on the Government by the likelihood that the whole story was about to be published in the United States.

Another

What puzzles M Ps is how it could take twelve years to learn that Philby was the third man, although he was sufficiently suspect to have been asked to resign from the Foreign Service only a few weeks after Burgess and Maclean disappeared.

Reports from America reached one or two M Ps last Thursday that another big spy scandal was about to break in Britain.

This was not the Philby case, but was reported to concern Polaris missiles.

Kim isn't here—Burgess

By FRANK DAWES

GUY BURGESS, the British diplomat who fled to Russia, roared with laughter last night when I spoke to him over the telephone to Moscow about Kim Philby.

He ridiculed Mr. Edward Heath's statement in the Commons that Philby was the "Third Man" in the sensational flight to Moscow by Burgess and Donald Maclean in 1951.

And Burgess denied any knowledge of journalist Philby being behind the Iron Curtain.

"Philby is an old friend of mine," he told me. "If he were here in Moscow—or even in Russia—he would certainly have given me a ring."

He added: "You know, my dear boy, the longer I stay in the Soviet Union and read about the Profumo scandal, the more glad I am to be here, and the more I believe that any civilised person, like Philby is, might even want to come here."

Of the Third Man mystery Burgess said: "There was no Third Man—unless it was the Special Branch themselves, giving themselves away. The truth is that Maclean, stopping in a taxi, was bumped into by a car carrying over-eager Special Branch sleuths.

"It was this, and this alone, which revealed to Maclean that he was being followed."

Of reports that Philby was a Soviet spy Burgess commented:

"He joined the Secret Service as my assistant. To my certain knowledge Kim was never a member of the Communist Party at Cambridge."

TWO GIRLS DROWN IN PIT

AN eight-year-old girl saw her elder sister and a friend drown in a flooded gravel pit yesterday.

The three girls had been gathering strawberries at Great Totham, near Maldon, Essex.

Ida Thoroughgood, aged 12, and her sister Mary, of Church Road, Wickham Bishops, Essex, cycled to Great Totham with Ida's 12-year-old friend Carol Carter, of The Wellands, Wickham Bishops.

On their way home they stopped to paddle in the 40ft-deep pit.

Carol fell into the water. Ida jumped into help. Neither of them could get back to the bank.

Mary ran off to dial 999 from the nearest phone. Workmen from a nearby building-site and police raced to the scene—but it was too late.

IRA man freed

The last I R A man detained in Britain, 38-year-old Joseph Doyle, was released from Wakefield prison yesterday.

'SOMEBODY IS SPREADING RUMOURS'

I'm not a ticket tout, says Pat

By PETER MOORHEAD

TENNIS star Pat Edrich, wife of Surrey and England batsman John Edrich, last night angrily denied rumours that she is involved in a ticket-tout racket.

The All-England Committee, who organise the Wimbledon tennis championships, have been told of a syndicate buying-up the books of six free tickets issued to each player.

The touts, said to be operating through a girl player, pay £10 for each book and resell it for £24.

'I know'

After being knocked out of a doubles match, Mrs. Edrich commented: "I've heard today that people are saying I am the girl mixed up with the syndicate. I want to deny it emphatically.

"I know the person who is spreading these tales. In fact, I heard this person speak to an official this morning and mention my name."

Mrs. Edrich, 29-year-old fashion model, added: "I'm not going to complain to the All-England Club about it at the moment. But if these rumours persist I will certainly take action."

Too hot

Major David Mills, secretary of the All-England Club, said last night: "I expect my committee will want to look into the matter. As far as I know no offence is committed by selling these tickets. But as they are gifts from the club they should on no account be sold."

Outside Wimbledon yesterday one spiv was selling Centre Court tickets for £5 a time and asking £15 each for finals tickets for Friday and Saturday.

PAT EDRICH
Test cricketer's wife

Astors home

Lord Astor and his wife, former fashion model Bronwen Pugh, arrived at London Airport last night after their five-day holiday in France. They left the Customs hall by a side exit.

'BULLIED GUARDS' INQUIRY

HERALD REPORTER

AN NCO in the Guards' depot at Pirbright, Surrey, has been posted to another unit following an inquiry into allegations that recruits had been bullied.

The depot's commandant, Lieut.-Colonel David Scott-Barrett, said last night: "As soon as I heard of the allegations, I ordered an immediate investigation.

"It looked as though only one NCO was responsible. He has been posted."

Colonel Scott-Barrett said he had no knowledge that recruits in the 14th company of Grenadier Guards had been struck on the head with rifle butts—a punishment nicknamed "Betsy."

'ISOLATED'

Nor had he heard of "knuckle sandwiches"—blows in the stomach.

He added: "The NCO who has been posted had been using wrong training methods. This was an isolated case.

"Guardsmen and recruits are under the most careful supervision at the depot. We will not tolerate bullying."

In March, 25 Scots Guardsmen walked out of Pirbright camp in protest at "excessive bull."

PAGE ONE SMILE

"Thank goodness they're going to abolish the 11-plus. It would have put years on me."

WEATHER

BRIGHT BUT COOL

COOL, cloudy and showery in most of Southern and Central England, but there will be some bright spells. Thunder is likely.

Midday temp.: 18 deg. C. (64 F.). **Outlook:** slightly warmer. **Lights:** 9.50 p.m. to 4.17 a.m. **High water London Bridge:** 12.2 a.m. **Yesterday's temp., Kew:** max. 20 deg. C. (68 F.); min. 12 deg. C. (54 F.). **Warmest:** Herne Bay 21 deg. C. (70 F.). **Coldest:** St. Abb's Head 11 deg. C. (52 F.). **Rainiest:** Skegness .69in. **Sunniest:** Tiree 10.8 hours. **Moon:** full July 6.

these promising men at the beginning of their careers, with the knowledge that they would eventually find employment in senior positions in British society. It was Blunt, as a young member of the teaching staff at Cambridge, who recruited Burgess and Maclean. The discovery that trusted men from "respectable" backgrounds could become traitors – Philby received an OBE (Order of the British Empire) for his wartime intelligence work, and Anthony Blunt was knighted after the war – shook British society.

Of the group only Harold "Kim" Philby was not a homosexual. Indeed, he enjoyed an active heterosexual life-style which took an unusual turn when Maclean's wife Melinda moved in with him in Moscow after he defected in 1963, before she finally returned to the United States. He was probably the most damaging of the group who served the Soviet Union for 30 years and was responsible for the death and disappearance of more loyal field men than any other Soviet agent.

Melinda, the American woman who was to become Maclean's wife, described him as "six foot four, blond, with beautiful eyes, altogether a beautiful man." Guy Burgess's description of a "large, flabby, white whale-like body" was less flattering. If Philby was sinister, Guy Francis de Moncy Burgess combined all the characteristics, bar greed, that could be exploited by a ruthless intelligence service. He was a drinker inclined to violence, a promiscuous homosexual, and a loyal believer in communism.

The members of the Cambridge spy

FAR LEFT: Harold "Kim" Philby's flight from Lebanon to the U.S.S.R. in January 1963 came as a shock to British society. He had held sensitive positions in MI6 and, after he had defected to the U.S.S.R., became an important member of the KGB's inner circle.

LEFT: Anthony Blunt, the "Fourth Man" of the Burgess, Maclean, Philby group, who was exposed in 1979. He had been knighted by the Queen for his work for art, and had been Surveyor of the Queen's Paintings, but he was stripped of his honor and died in 1983 at the age of 76. During an interview after he had been exposed, Blunt said, "I did not betray my conscience," but there was little public sympathy for a man who had enjoyed a privileged life.

LEFT: Benedict Arnold is a name which is almost synonymous with treason for many Americans, but from a British perspective he could be regarded as a useful "asset" in their war with the rebellious colonists of America.

ring were not men who took up spying to supplement their salaries. They had well-paid jobs in the security services or diplomatic corps. The drinking and homosexuality of Burgess and Maclean may have raised some eyebrows, but the style was public enough that it could not be seen as a security threat. The left-wing politics and commitment to the Soviet Union which secretly sustained them were long forgotten in their student past. These men would have been classified by Sun Tzu Wu as converted spies, valuable assets who merited attention and respect.

These men were, of course, by no means the first traitors to make their mark on history. Their activities represent an age-old phenomenon. The most notorious traitor in the history of the United States, until the Rosenbergs,

must be Benedict Arnold, who in September 1780 commanded the American revolutionary garrison at West Point on the Hudson River. Working through the British Major John André, he sent word that he was prepared to deliver the position to General Sir William Clinton. Arnold, as a good British asset, was rewarded with a Brigadier General's promotion and a substantial cash reward, and thereafter he fought for the British. His "case officer," Major André, was captured with the plans of West Point by revolutionary forces and hanged as a spy, a fate he did not deserve, but which he accepted with a dignity that impressed his captors.

Another famous spy who faced her death with dignity was the World War I femme fatale Mata Hari. Executed by the French at Vincennes, this exotic dancer

RIGHT: Mata Hari, in more conventional attire, before World War I. In the Cold War her espionage, which was little more than indiscreet gossip, would have merited a short time in prison, not execution — the fate she suffered in World War I.

was probably more of a gossip that a spy, but fell victim to the paranoia and suspicion generated in World War I. At her trial in 1917 she was found guilty on eight charges of passing information of interest to Arnold Kalle, the German naval attaché in Madrid, but this had no real military or political value. It was never proved that she had surreptitiously gathered news from her French, Belgian, Dutch, or British lovers to sell to the enemy. She admitted that she had received money from Cramer, the German Consul in Amsterdam, as an advance payment for information, but claimed she had supplied none.

Her stage name, Malay for "eve of the day," disguised her origins: she was born Margaretha Geertruida Zelle in a small Frisian town in the Netherlands. It was her marriage to a Dutch officer who had served in the East Indies that gave her the idea of "Hindu Dancing." She enjoyed a considerable following as a dancer

before the war, and after August 1914 was able to travel to neutral countries in the course of her career. It was these overseas trips that were her undoing. Her execution by a firing squad from the 4th Regiment of Zouaves, was both brave and dignified. In Cell 12 at Saint-Lazaire she dressed in a pearl-gray frock, slung a coat over her shoulders, and donned a dark tricornered hat with veil, and gloves. She refused a blindfold and stood straight rather than have her hands lashed to the post. She thanked the lieutenant, sergeant major, and firing squad, and as they raised their rifles she lifted her hands and blew them a kiss. After the shots were fired, she crumpled into what one witness described as "a heap of petticoats." She was not buried – the French military gave her body to a teaching hospital for dissection.

ABOVE: Major John André, still clad in his soldier's red coat, which he wore while operating behind rebel lines, is hanged by the Americans following his capture during the Revolution. André was Arnold's "case officer" and hardly deserved to be executed.

THE MISSIONS

Intelligence-gathering missions can be enormously varied, but all originate from a requirement for "basic intelligence." The most comprehensive definition of this term is that of the U.S. DoD.

Fundamental intelligence concerning the general situation, resources, capabilities, and vulnerabilities of foreign countries or areas which may be used as reference material in the planning of operations at any level and in evaluating subsequent information relating to the same subject.

The intelligence can in turn be broken down into long-term and short-term. Long-term may concern future economic, diplomatic, or military plans, or major weapons-development programs, and is built up from a mixture of classified and public sources as well as from the calculated judgments of defense and intelligence analysts. The DoD and NATO call this type of intelligence "strategic," and the DoD defines it as:

Intelligence that is required for the formation of policy and military plans at national and international levels. Strategic intelligence and tactical intelligence differ primarily in level of application but may also vary in terms of scope and detail.

It can also include the personalities of military, political, and commercial leaders and, more significantly, the up-and-coming leaders in these fields.

Warsaw Pact and Soviet intelligence agencies placed considerable emphasis on HUMINT. Senior commanders in the East German National Volksarmee (NVA), for example, were required to know the biographical profile of their NATO opposite number. However, Field Marshal Montgomery anticipated this approach by having the portraits of Rommel and Model, his two major adversaries in World War II, on the wall of his personal command trailer. The KGB and GRU (State Intelligence Department) penetration of Western agencies often relied on HUMINT and, in the case of the Cambridge spy ring, on a shrewd assessment of the individuals who would eventually hold senior political and intelligence positions in the British government.

HUMINT need not have a purely military application. In international diplomatic negotiations it is valuable for the major players to have a detailed background on the character of the individuals they will meet across the conference table. It may also be possible to intercept the signals they are sending back to their domestic governments and gain an insight into how they see the negotiations developing.

An intriguing aspect of Soviet HUMINT operations was revealed in June 1993 when, at a conference to mark the 75th year of the Pontifical Institute of Oriental Studies in the Vatican, Father Clarence Gallagher admitted that some seminarians, particularly those from Eastern Europe, had gathered intelligence for the KGB. *Newsweek* reported: "Some of the spies may have had a

RIGHT: Soviet premier Nikita Khrushchev, during a visit to the United States in 1959, with President Dwight D. Eisenhower. During the visit Khrushchev agreed to negotiate further on Berlin, which, until 1989, was one of the potential "hot spots" in the world, though with détente in the 1970s and 1980s it became a less sensitive issue.

genuine priestly vocation; information gathering may have been the price they paid Soviet authorities to practice their faith. Others may have been out-and-out frauds. The Vatican is not saying what it will do to unmask them. This is one case in which the confessional is unlikely to be much help."

Short-term intelligence can be as immediate as a promptly reported telephone call about a person under surveillance. Unlike long-term intelligence, which may be built up over years before it reaches useful maturity, short-term may have a very brief useful life. This type of information is sometimes called "current intelligence," and is defined by the DoD and IADB as:

Intelligence of all types and forms of immediate interest which is usually disseminated without the delays necessary to complete evaluation of interpretation.

In this respect it is the type of information which in an operational military context would be used from brigade downward, and is akin to "combat information," which NATO defines as:

that frequently perishable data gathered in combat by, or reported to, units which may be immediately used in battle or in assessing the situation.

ABOVE: "Kim" Philby covering the Spanish Civil War as a journalist from the Fascist lines after he was lightly wounded by shellfire in 1937. His "Fascist" sympathies were part of a cover developed by the Soviets.

LEFT: U.S. Special Forces officers with Vietnamese "Strikers" – members of the Strike Team – question suspect Vietcong in 1966. The Special Forces, or Green Berets, were a useful instrument of U.S. policy in the 1960s when they were operating as advisers to Third World governments who claimed to be under threat from Communists.

BELOW: A Phoenix Unmanned Air Vehicle (UAV) in service with the British Army to give "real time" battlefield intelligence for artillery, including Multiple Launch Rocket Systems (MLRS).

In a counterterrorist campaign, this type of information can be as immediate as a local contact saying to a security-force patrol, "Don't go down that road, I think they've set an ambush."

Information which has been evaluated by analysts becomes "combat intelligence." This type of intelligence may have come in through front-line prisoner-of-war (PoW) interrogation or conversations with the local population, reports by reconnaissance patrols or artillery observation posts, film or photographs from aircraft or Remotely Piloted Vehicle (RPV) flights, or even something as simple as a commander making a close study of his map. Under these circumstances, the intelligence will be acted on, but also logged for transmission up the chain of command, since it may help to build up the larger long-term intelligence picture.

Interestingly, another subgroup exists beside combat intelligence. This is called "tactical intelligence," and is generally intelligence which is required for the planning and conduct of tactical operations. In this field another type of short-term intelligence is "target intelligence" – it might be assumed that this would be used exclusively by special forces raiding parties or bomber/ground-attack aircrew since it is "intelligence which portrays and locates the components of a target or target complex and indicates its vulnerability and relative importance." However, during the Cold War, NATO combat engineers had detailed information on all the bridges in West Germany, as well as other communications bottlenecks which could be demolished to impede a Soviet and Warsaw Pact mechanized advance. In addition there were detailed "going" maps showing the type of terrain – rocky, soft soil, slopes, or woodland. These could be used to plan the siting of defensive positions or routes for counterattacks.

In a counterterrorist campaign, or where there is a threat from hostile special forces, short-term and long-term intelligence can be used to build up a "security intelligence" picture. This intelligence on the identity, capabilities, and intentions of hostile organizations or individuals who are, or may be, engaged in espionage, sabotage, subversion or terrorism can include the education and family background of a suspect. If, for example, a young man has electrical or electronic training, then he has the capability to be a bomber, and although the neighbors and members of a family of a known terrorist may not have criminal records, they may be tacit supporters of terrorist organizations.

Clearly, information gathered under the title of security intelligence has the potential to be used by unprincipled authorities to spy on legitimate parties or groups politically opposed to their government. Though the operations of the KGB in the former Soviet Union are seen as one of the worst examples of internal repression by the organs of state security, the work of the MfS (Ministerium für Staatssicherheit), the Ministry of State Security, dominated the lives of all who lived in East Germany. With the opening of government files following unification in November 1989, a complex web of surveillance, both freelance and professional, has been revealed, with detailed files being held on many East German citizens.

Internal surveillance and repression is, of course, equally prevalent in many right-wing governments. Before and during World War II the Fascist governments of both Germany, and to a lesser extent Italy, used their security services to dominate not only their own countries, but also those they conquered and occupied. In the 1970s and early 1980s the police and intelligence services of the military governments of Argentina, Chile, and Peru, among others, conducted ruthless campaigns against left-wing groups and terrorist organizations. In Argentina the security forces short-circuited the legal process by simply kidnapping suspects and "disappearing" them. These men and women were never heard of again. What in fact happened was that they were tortured and interrogated and then murdered – their bodies being dumped in the Rio Plata river or in anonymous graves. This type of operation had its origins in Stalin's U.S.S.R., where "enemies of the state" were executed and dumped in mass graves, and in Nazi Germany, where those arrested were described as having disappeared into the "*nacht und nebel*" – the night and fog.

The fight against the illegal drug trade has given security intelligence a new and important role. Columbia, Peru, Central Asia, and the Far East, as the main suppliers, have become the targets for penetration and intelligence gathering. Admiral Bobby Ray Inman, the youthful former director of the CIA, highlighted the character of state-sponsored terrorism and the narcotics trade. They "are not played by the gentlemanly rules of the espionage world. When you try to penetrate them and they suspect you, they don't put you in jail. They shoot."

Security intelligence can also include the background on diplomats or members

BELOW: President Augusto Pinochet in 1987 after signing into effect a law which permitted the formation of non-Marxist political parties. Both Chile and Argentina waged internal wars against Communist organizations.

ABOVE: A U.S. secret service agent with a sub-machine gun concealed in his shoulder bag and radio earpiece in place, as well as a pistol on his belt, guards the presidential Black Hawk helicopter as President George Bush arrives at an anti-drugs conference at Cartagena, Colombia, in February 1990.

of trade missions who, in the old Soviet terminology, are "legal" residents in a country. They have a "front" function, but are in reality conducting espionage operations within their host country. "Illegals" are agents who do not have diplomatic protection, and, if caught, will be tried and sentenced. During the Cold War the Soviet "legal" structure in London was twice decimated, with expulsions of 105 embassy and trade legation staff in 1971, and 62 in 1983. Among the men expelled in 1971 was Alexander Gresko who had been caught red-handed trying to bribe science writers to get secret technical information. He was given a new mission by his Soviet masters as the political escort for Soviet athletes, including Olga Korbut, the petite gymnast who entranced the world in the late 1970s. He managed to make all her interviews sound like Soviet propaganda, but because of his past, he failed to win a post at the 1976 Montreal Olympics as an "Olympic attaché."

At the opposite end of the scale from HUMINT are a cluster of electronic intelligence initials: ELINT, ELECTRO-OPINT, COMINT, and SIGINT. All of these forms of intelligence gathering were important during the Cold War, with both NATO and the Warsaw Pact operating elaborate listening posts across their territories. Hopefully, all of these bases have become redundant with the fall of the Berlin Wall, the reunification of Germany, and the tentative return of democracy to Eastern Europe.

In their time the Danish island of Bornholm in the Baltic and the Teufelberge, the artificial hills made from the rubble of bombed Berlin, had elaborate listening devices. Bornholm's interception equipment was so comprehensive that it was said to be able to "look down the throat of the Warsaw Pact." On the Brocken Mountain, on the East German border south of Braunschweig, there was a 2750-foot-high Soviet and East German listening station.

LEFT: A Soviet UAZ vehicle in Kunashir in 1989 passes a complex of tracking radars which would give advanced warning of hostile aircraft. Kunashir is an island just off Japan's northernmost main island of Hokkaido.

RIGHT: A U.S. Marine Corps AV-8B Harrier attack aircraft fitted with a GEC-Marconi forward-looking infrared (FLIR) sensor immediately in front of the cockpit. FLIR allows the aircraft to operate at night and, unlike radar, is a passive system which cannot be detected.

One U.S. Army interpreter recalled a night when the U.S. Berlin listening posts were galvanized by a garbled radio conversation between two senior Soviet officers who were commanding tank units in a major exercise in East Germany. The tape-recorded conversation was very unclear, with static and electronic "mush." However, the American crew could clearly hear the words "Third World War." It was only by patiently listening to the tape, phrase by phrase, that they teased out the full text of the conversation. It went, "if this exercise is due to run for an extra three days it will be Third World War, when I get home to my wife."

At sea Soviet fishing vessels with an unnecessary surplus of radio antennae would shadow NATO exercises, or long-range Tu-20 Bear-D bombers equipped with ESM/ECM pods and antennae would overfly NATO carriers during the takeoff and landing of aircraft.

Though the Cold War has ended, monitoring continues from a number of locations – Cyprus is particularly useful as a monitoring base for the West because it allows radio signals from the Middle East to be taped and analyzed.

ELINT, or electronic intelligence, is defined by the DoD and IADB as:

technical and intelligence information derived from foreign non-communications electromagnetic radiations emanating from other than nuclear detonations or radioactive sources.

All these intelligence-gathering operations were based on systems like radars or laser range-finders, which could be intercepted and analyzed. Knowledge of the frequencies of hostile radars can be invaluable – the Israelis have made considerable efforts to learn about Syrian air-defense radars and those used in naval surface-to-surface missiles. In the Peace for Galilee operations in June 1982, RPVs were used to penetrate the Bekaa Valley in Lebanon to locate Syrian SAM (surface-to-air missile) positions and jam radars. Earlier, in the Vietnam War, U.S. Air Force aircraft on "Wild Weasel" missions (operations to

ABOVE: The antenna of the Ballistic Missile Early Warning System (BMEWS) at Thule, Greenland. Systems like BMEWS were intended to give warning so that retaliatory missile strikes could be launched before U.S. cities and missile silos were destroyed by incoming Soviet missiles.

suppress North Vietnam's air-defense systems) had stalked SAMs with radar-homing AGM-45 Shrike missiles. The missiles followed the beams from the Vietnamese radars trying to locate U.S. aircraft, thereby hitting the target with great accuracy. Like the subsequent "Black Buck" raids by the RAF against Argentine radar positions on the Falklands in 1982, it was a cat-and-mouse operation. Each side knew that operating the air-defense radar could mean the death of the aircraft crew or the radar technicians. Similar episodes occurred during the Gulf War.

When night-vision equipment is used the process is known as ELECTRO-OPINT, which is defined by the DoD as:

intelligence information other than signals intelligence derived from the optical monitoring of the electromagnetic spectrum from ultraviolet through far infrared.

The interception and analysis of radio signals is called COMINT, or communications intelligence, and is defined as:

technical and intelligence information derived from foreign communications by other than the intended recipients.

SIGINT, or signals intelligence, is a more detailed definition and includes U.S. DoD subdefinitions like SIGINT direct service, SIGINT operational control, SIGINT resources, and SIGINT support plans. SIGINT itself is a category of intelligence comprising all communications intelligence, electronics intelligence, and telemetry intelligence. In order to defeat intelligence gathering through SIGINT, modern radios and communications equipment have been fitted with electronic countermeasures. Frequency-agile or frequency-hopping countermeasures are particularly effective, and work by changing the frequency

ABOVE: A Racal armored fighting vehicle radio; frequency-agile radios allow tank crews to communicate securely without having to encrypt messages manually. This in turn makes armored operations faster as well as more secure.

ABOVE: Bletchley Park, Buckinghamshire, England, the wartime home of the Government Code and Cypher School where Ultra decryption of German Enigma signals were conducted. This operation did much to shape Allied military operations.

LEFT: General Heinz Guderian in his SdKfz 251 command half-track during the invasion of France in May 1940. Two signalers in the foreground are operating the Enigma. Some photographs show the equipment, which looked rather like a typewriter, but others, like this one, have been cropped to conceal it. The Germans relied heavily on Enigma, as they believed it to be totally secure. This made them very vulnerable to SIGINT analysis by the Allies.

so rapidly that only very small fragments of a transmission can be detected.

The other answer is encryption, which makes the transmission sound like a jumble of incomprehensible noises. Encryption, which consists of two devices, one which jumbles up the sound of the human voice at transmission and another at reception which reassembles them, is increasingly favored for portable telephones. Senior CIA officers have ruefully commented that advances in the field of encryption by companies looking for private buyers may pose a problem for security and civil rights.

If there are no electronic aids to ensure security, operators may use simple, but secure, one-time code pads. Simple one-time codes are almost impossible to break since only a small number of people will have the preformatted pads, but their use takes time and patience. Electronic encryption is clearly the answer, since it is fast and almost unbreakable. However, as the Ultra operation in World War II showed, as well as the Walker spy ring in the 1980s, even electronic systems can be penetrated by ability or treachery.

The disadvantage of coded transmissions is that the monitoring of radio traffic from a station will give hostile listeners an idea of both its importance, and, by using direction-finding equipment, its location. In a battlefield, this would ensure the destruction of the station if the indications (usually volume of transmissions) were that it was part of a headquarters complex. Modern electronic warfare systems will provide a computer-generated map of the area in which the radio stations are located, and this in turn will allow intelligence officers to build up a clearer picture of the enemy operation.

Frequency-hopping radios are one solution to this problem and do away with the need to encrypt; another solution, however, is burst transmission. Here, a message is formatted in a simple alpha-numeric code, and this is transmitted at high speed, so that it is impossible to detect, let alone intercept. The alphanumeric code is essential, since a cluster of words and letters will stand for a quite complex message onto which a few figures can be added.

While transmissions were one way of deriving information about enemy electronic equipment, photographs taken from the air, space, and even on the ground were studied closely. The shape of radio or radar antennae give some indication of their function – search, air-

traffic control, missile-guidance radars, or HF sky-wave antennae. Jamie Jameson, who was a senior officer with the CIA in Europe, recalled at a conference held by the International Freedom Foundation in 1991 in Washington an unlikely combination of HUMINT and TECHINT – technical intelligence. In the 1950s and '60s about 5-6000 young Spaniards, who as children of Communist sympathizers had escaped at the end of the Civil War and gone to the U.S.S.R., returned to Spain. The CIA had a requirement to know about a new Soviet radar that had a rotating antenna with an over-the-horizon capability. Jameson explained how

ABOVE: The Enigma encryption machine was portable, and apparently totally secure. It was based on prewar commercial machines which could be used for secure business communication. The Ultra operation cracked the system with some fine mathematical brains, as well as with information collected by the French and Polish secret services.

the CIA acquired this information.

One of these things had been seen by some attaché, but he was not really sure if he had actually seen it – it was very much in doubt. The existence of the radar was pinned down by a young Spanish lady, who was rather comely in appearance and decided to supplement her normal income, which was rather low in a small village outside Moscow, by accommodating the lust of local airmen at an air base there. She apparently earned a large amount of her money lying down and looking upward in the evening, and was able, because she did most of her business under one of these great big radars, to give us a very accurate description of the configurations of these big rotating antennae. She really did not have her mind on her other work I guess.

The intense Soviet and Warsaw Pact interest in Western technology could, of course, lead to spoofs, either by design, or

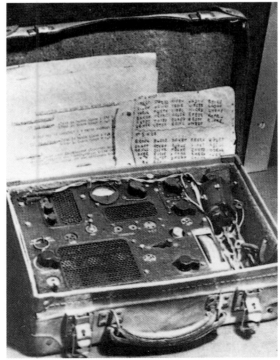

ABOVE: A Kriegsmarine radio operator on a U-boat encrypts a signal using his Enigma machine, which can be seen at the lower left of the photograph. The Allied war against the U-boats used Ultra intelligence, though of the three German services the Kriegsmarine was the most thorough with its signals security.

LEFT: A small portable Mark III transceiver used by Allied agents in occupied Europe. Operators used Morse since it was a more reliable way of communicating in difficult electronic conditions.

simply because soldiers become bored and have a sense of humor. A British Army border patrol on the Inner German Border (IGB) between East and West Germany realized that it was under photographic surveillance by the Kommando Grenze East German border guards in their watchtowers. One morning the photography became particularly active, since the guards had spotted a new piece of electronic equipment mounted on the front fender of a British Land Rover. This was comprehensively covered by long-range photography, with a view to subsequent analysis. The East Germans probably never realized that the "equipment" was, in fact, a jumbo-sized breakfast cereal box, sprayed olive drab and fitted with an "antenna" made from an unwound wire coat hanger. The Norwegian border troops in the far north achieved a similar effect with a broom handle and a curved strip of cardboard – the Soviet KGB border guards were intrigued by what appeared to be a compact vehicle-mounted radar.

The Soviet and Warsaw Pact forces were at pains to cover or conceal with tarpaulin equipment which might be photographed. With developments in satellite photography, concealment became even more important. The process of guessing from a photograph what type of weapon or equipment was under a tarpaulin cover became known jokingly as "tarpaulogy."

In contrast to the battlefield intelligence derived from intercepts and photographs, there is the more erudite area of scientific and technical intelligence, which is often abbreviated to TECHINT and is defined by the DoD and IADB as:

The product resulting from the collection, evaluation, analysis, and interpretation of foreign scientific and technical information which covers: (a) foreign developments in basic and applied research and in applied engineering techniques; and (b) scientific and technical characteristics, capabilities, and limitations of all foreign military systems, weapons, weapons systems, and material, the research and development related thereto, and the production methods employed for their manufacture.

The nascent Soviet Union placed considerable weight on the value of TECHINT and established a directorate for scientific and technical intelligence in 1925. Even following the collapse of the U.S.S.R., Russia is still conducting TECHINT operations. In August 1992 the Japanese declared Vladimir Davydov

persona non grata. Davydov, a trade representative in the embassy in Tokyo, was charged, with a Japanese associate, with trying to obtain semiconductors and telecommunications equipment which were banned from export.

Unquestionably, however, the most significant TECHINT espionage operation of the postwar years was undertaken by Klaus Fuchs, a German Communist physicist who had worked both on Tube Alloys, the British atomic weapons research project, and subsequently the

ABOVE: A Royal Artillery Javelin missile crew with a radio fitted with a data-burst transmission system. This allows information to be pre-formatted and sent at very high speed so that it cannot be detected.

LEFT: Harry Gold, between two guards. Gold was the contact between the atomic-weapons spy Klaus Fuchs and Anatoli Yakovlev, a GRU officer. After his arrest Gold was cooperative and provided evidence against David Greenglass and the Rosenbergs. He was sentenced to 30 years imprisonment, but was paroled in 1965 and returned to Philadelphia where he died seven years later aged 60.

BELOW: Congressional Atomic Committee chiefs read of Fuchs' arrest. Senator Brien McMahon (left) Chairman of the Joint Congressional Atomic Committee and Vice Chairman Carl T. Durham are seen at an emergency meeting called by McMahon to discuss the arrest and its implications.

Manhattan Project, the U.S. program. For two and a half years he passed details of the research in the United States to Harry Gold, who was working for Anatoli Yakovlev, a GRU officer working under the cover of the Soviet Consul in New York. Fuchs returned to the United Kingdom after the war and was appointed head of theoretical physics at the Atomic Energy Establishment at Harwell. Ironically, when in 1950 Fuchs was questioned by William Skardon, an experienced MI5 interrogator, and gave a detailed confession of his treachery, he was deeply saddened to discover that he would lose his British citizenship and his post at Harwell, both of which he had grown to value greatly.

Found guilty, Fuchs was sentenced to 14 years in prison – the maximum penalty. He served nine, and upon release moved to East Germany. Significantly, his motives for spying were ideological, which made him harder to detect. Gold, his contact in the United States, was sentenced to 30 years, but was paroled in 1965 and returned to Philadelphia, where he died seven years later at the age of 60. The Soviet government rewarded him with the Order of the Red Star. In the words of Christopher Dobson and Ronald Payne in *The Dictionary of Espionage*, "this entitled him among other things to free rides on the buses in

Moscow, a privilege which, as J. Edgar Hoover tartly remarked, he was never destined to enjoy."

Of the atomic-bomb spies only the Rosenbergs paid the ultimate penalty. They were children of Jewish immigrants who had settled in New York. Julius had become a Communist in his youth but after graduating in electrical engineering he ceased his public political life to work for Anatoli Yakovlev. Initially the Rosenbergs were not major players in the atomic-bomb spy ring; however, their flat became a clearing house for "dead-letter drops," and they recruited agents. The case for the prosecution of the Rosenbergs hinged on the evidence of Harry Gold and David Greenglass, the brother of Ethel. A deal allowed the wife of Greenglass to escape prosecution in return for the evidence her husband supplied against his sister. It seems evident that Ethel was arrested and prosecuted to bring pressure to bear on Julius, but both protested their innocence to the electric chair.

The execution of the Rosenbergs in 1953 started a controversy that lasted

LEFT: David Greenglass was a former U.S. Army NCO who passed information from Klaus Fuchs to Soviet intelligence. When arrested, he was prepared to testify against his sister, Ethel Rosenberg, to protect his wife, Ruth. He was sentenced to 15 years imprisonment, but only served two-thirds of the sentence. After his release he changed his name to preserve his privacy.

BELOW: Julius and Ethel Rosenberg leave the Federal Court after their conviction on charges of espionage and conspiracy on March 29, 1951. Critics say that the evidence against Ethel was slim and that she was arrested to bring pressure to bear on Julius.

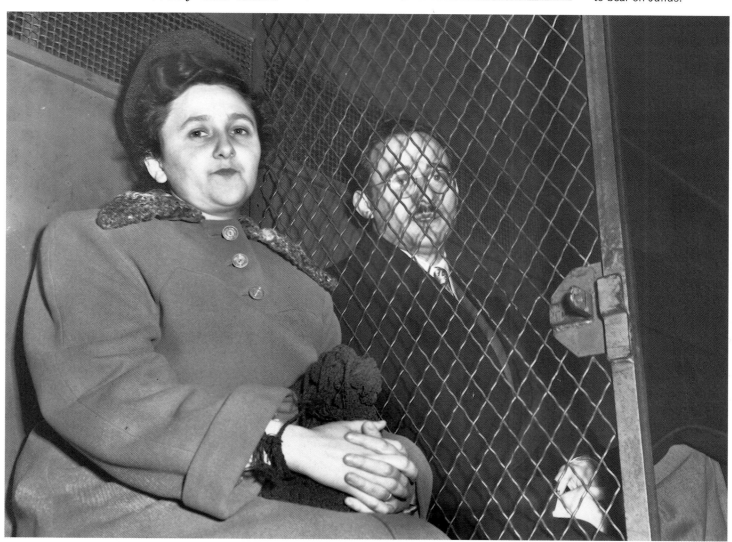

LEFT: Protesters outside the White House on February 17, 1953 argue the case for and against the Rosenberg execution. The Rosenbergs' death sentence was in part a result of the anti-Communist sentiment generated by the Korean War. Appeals against the death sentence went as high as President Dwight D. Eisenhower.

many years – were they victims of a frame-up, and was the death sentence justified? Of the death sentence, it must be said that the climate of the times was tough – the Korean War was raging and Czechoslovakia had been seized by the Communists. Public opinion and attitudes toward spies and Communists was not as pragmatic as it was to become between the 1960s and the 1980s. Moreover, all the due processes of the law were observed, with appeals going as high as President Eisenhower. Thirty years later, the FBI files revealed that though the Rosenbergs may not have been effective spies, Julius made every effort to provide high-grade information, and his material was a useful double-check against information coming from other sources like Klaus Fuchs.

Two agents who escaped to Mexico before the Yakovlev spy ring collapsed were Morris Cohen and his wife Lona. Under the names Peter and Helen Kroger, and a cover that they were Canadian, they surfaced in London as "illegals" and ran communications for what was known as the Portland spy ring. The Soviet government claimed that the Cohen-Krogers were, in fact, Poles, and so this prevented them from being deported back to the United States. They were sentenced by the British to 20 years imprisonment, but were exchanged

for Gerald Brooke, a lecturer held in the U.S.S.R. for distributing subversive literature. Peter Kroger's last words on British soil were, "ta-ta and say goodbye for me to all the lads in Parkhurst" – Parkhurst is a high-security jail on the Isle of Wight, off the south coast of England.

As Soviet industrial capability and expertise began to decline in the mid-1970s, its secret services were given the task of gathering technical information about a wide range of subjects. One of the more bizarre KGB operations involved an attempt to suborn a Norwegian oilman, Sven Erling Haugen. When he realized that he had been targeted, he at once contacted the Norwegian

ABOVE: An altercation outside the funeral home in Brooklyn, New York, at the Rosenberg funeral. Julius had considered becoming a rabbi, but had rejected religion for communism.

security services, and for seven years passed carefully "sanitized" information to the KGB.

Christopher Dobson and Ronald Payne describe how the first contact was made with Haugen. The Norwegian oilman was manning a stand at the North Sea Exhibition in Stavanger, Norway, when Alexander Dementiev, a KGB officer working under the cover of the Soviet trade delegation in Oslo, engaged him in conversation about the Stratfjord A platform, which was under construction. A series of business lunches followed with several small presents. Eventually Dementiev began paying $1500 for information. Haugen had to sign for the payments, but the KGB man took a cut of between 10 and 15 percent.

The demand for information increased and included target intelligence for attacks on Western oil platforms, as well as technical intelligence that the Soviet Union could exploit for its own exploration operations. Alexander Dementiev was expelled from Oslo in 1977, and Haugen thought that this would be the end of his operations. However, a year later, the Norwegian received an invitation to Vienna from Dementiev. Cash passed hands, with the usual cut, and then Haugen was passed to a new handler. The new man, Dr. Arkadu Belozerov, was a KGB colonel, and if Dementiev was crude, Belozerov was bumbling. He would arrange to meet at a restaurant – but they would arrive and find that it was closed. When they found a restaurant, he took the technical papers and hurried out to deliver them to a waiting car which was to rush to the embassy for photocopying – the trouble was that he could not find the car.

Despite this clumsiness, Belozerov had very detailed information requirements, even giving the index numbers of technical papers. Belozerov's cover was as a secretary at the International Institute of Applied Systems Analysis in Vienna. The institute had been set up as a confidence-building gesture by President Lyndon Johnson and Dzermen Givishiani, the son-in-law of Soviet premier Alexei Kosygin. Eventually, by April 1981, the Norwegian intelligence service felt that, having penetrated KGB opera-

BELOW: In a protest near Union Square, 5000 Rosenberg sympathizers branded the execution as "murder." Even now, after 30 years, it is still controversial, and if the Rosenbergs had been convicted later in the Cold War, they would probably have just received long prison sentences.

tions in Oslo and Vienna, they had achieved enough, and so the operation ended with simple announcements that T. A. Besidin, a trade-delegation official, G. G. Petrov, and E. S. Mirinenko were *personae non grata*. Arkady Belozerov left Vienna two weeks later, stating, "I deny the charges completely, but the accusations may disturb the spirit of the Institute, therefore I have decided regretfully to offer my resignation."

Speaking in the summer of 1993, Yuri Kobaladze, spokesman for the Russian Foreign Intelligence Service – in effect the successor of the KGB – said, "Economic intelligence has nothing to do with the stealing of secrets. It is analysis of information."

What distinguishes TECHINT operations of the 1990s from those of the Cold-War years is that they are conducted between nations that are "friends." Gaining an edge on the international competition either by overt or covert means can make a huge difference to designers or manufacturers of high-technology equipment. In its June 7, 1993 issue, *Time* magazine described how, in March, a 21-page document arrived at the U.S. Embassy in Paris. It "amounted to a virtual shopping list of U.S. industrial 'targets' for French intelligence agents, including 49 American high-tec firms, 24 banks and brokerage houses, and four U.S. government agencies." The intelligence directive was drafted by the Exploitation-Implementation Office of the Department of Economics, Science, and Technology, a branch of the Direction General de la Sécurité Extérieure

(DGSE), France's foreign-intelligence service. A month later in an interview, Claude Silberzahn, head of DGSE, admitted that "today's espionage is essentially economic, scientific, technological, and financial." The CIA warned U.S. manufacturers exhibiting at the Paris Air Show in 1993 that they would be targets for the DGSE, and this prompted Hughes Aircraft to stay at home and Pratt & Whitney not to display its technological showpiece, a new tilting-nozzle jet engine.

In the new world of economic espionage, France is at an advantage, since it has large, state-controlled or government-funded manufacturers like Bull, Dassault, Renault, and Thomson CSF. Speaking at "Assessing U.S. Intelligence Needs for the 1990s," a series of seminars held in Washington, Theodore Shackley, a veteran CIA officer, identified the

problem for the United States.

If the U.S. had acquired some data on a very large project . . . and there were only two American firms that were competing, and all of the others were German, British, French, and so forth, it would be possible to take that data, call in those two American companies, and share it simultaneously with them through the Treasury Department, or through the Commerce Department. . . . On the other hand, if you find out something that is really unique about computers, and microchips, who do you call in from Silicon Valley? How do you disseminate that information to a variety of American companies that permits them to get a competitive edge?

French interest in the United States dates back to the 1960s. In 1989 the FBI and U.S. intelligence agencies broke up a

LEFT: A member of a Soviet industrial spy ring operating in West Germany in the mid-1960s, climbs a tree to collect material left in a "dead-letter box." The ring consisted of two newsmen and three members of a trade mission, all of whom would have been able to make a case for having access to industrial information.

ABOVE: A Soviet-made Romanian Air Force MIG-21 on display at the Paris Air Show at Le Bourget. It is being upgraded by Israel Aircraft Industries and ELTA. The airframe is well known, but upgrades like enhanced avionics would be of interest to industrial spies from both East and West.

network of dozens of agents of the DGSE who had penetrated several major U.S. companies, including IBM, Texas Instruments, and Corning. For two years they had been sending marketing plans, financial information, and data on computer and fiber-optics technology to such firms as Compagnie des Machines Bull, which *Time* described as "France's chronically less-than-competitive computer maker."

Among the other targets for French economic intelligence-gathering operations were the Bell/Boeing V-22 Osprey, a revolutionary tilt-rotor aircraft, and Motorola's cellular-telephone marketing strategy for penetrating Europe. In July 1990 a Frenchman was convicted of stealing documents from Renaissance Software, a Californian firm. In December 1991 six French engineers visiting the U.S. were pressured into leaving, after showing too much interest in Stealth research. Posing as nuclear engineers trying to develop nuclear-safety technology, they had instead tried to obtain samples of the coatings used on Stealth aircraft, such as the F-117 and B-2. According to Jay Branegan writing in *Time*, "DGSE officials categorically deny the agency's involvement in either case."

France is not alone in waging this type of undeclared war. It is believed that the Japanese intelligence arm MITI has an organization called JETRO which collects economic information. "They share it," says Theodore Shackley, "on a rather arbitrary, capricious manner with those companies that they favor at a particular moment." One estimate puts Japan's commitment to industrial espionage at 80 percent of its intelligence-gathering resources. China is also keen to catch up with the West, by fair means or foul. At ASIANDEX, a defense-equipment exhibition held in Beijing, British exhibitors claimed that their equipment on display had clearly been tampered with and examined overnight. One combat-radio manufacturer had the shrewd good sense to bring radios which had only the external controls and none of the internal "guts" – they were, in effect, just empty green boxes.

In 1992 Russian spies were expelled or exposed in Belgium, France, Italy, and the Netherlands. British sources estimate that about half the 56 Russian spies active in Britain are involved in industrial and high-tech espionage. French counterintelligence officers assert that 80 percent of today's economic intelligence gathering can be done by analyzing public sources like academic journals, industrial publications, company brochures, and computer databases. However, writing in *Time*, Bruce W. Nelan comments, "Valuable secrets can usually be stolen only by traditional tactics: bribery, burglary [and] infiltration."

BELOW: A prototype of the world's first production tilt-rotor aircraft, the Bell-Boeing V-22 Osprey. There were reports that the French aviation industry was particularly interested in its design.

THE MEANS

One of the most dramatic developments in espionage equipment in the late-twentieth century is to be found in almost all offices in most major cities. The photocopier has allowed classified documents to be copied quickly and cleanly. The old world of clandestine nocturnal or lunch-break visits with miniature cameras to government offices, has been replaced by the junior staff apparently making some legitimate copies of a document during the working day.

As the previous chapter showed, intelligence-gathering operations are moving away from military plans, or weapons research and development programs, to industrial, economic, or political information. In this respect much of the equipment developed during the Cold War has less relevance. Satellite and aerial photography was essential when the Soviet Union was a closed society which could use its huge land mass to conceal factories, vehicle parks, radar installations, and missile or nuclear weapons tests. There was a boast that the quality of the photography was so good that it could show vehicle license plates.

Satellite intelligence has been used in several "hot" wars since its inception. The latest was the Gulf War of 1990-91 in which satellite imagery allowed tanks, vehicles, and positions to be plotted in the Iraqi and Kuwaiti desert. Electronic-warfare eavesdropping equipment was another area of development. It was so sophisticated that, reportedly, it was able to intercept short-wave radio conversations between the chauffeurs of party offi-

cials in Moscow from beyond the borders of the U.S.S.R. Radio listening stations exist around the borders of the Warsaw Pact countries, China, and the Middle East. Those monitoring China and the Middle East continue to be important. Interestingly, not all of the information gathered by electronic means is military radio traffic; it can be internal or overseas radio and TV broadcasts.

There was considerable debate during the Gulf War about how much intelligence or disinformation was being aired through the medium of television. On a routine basis, intercepts of Middle East radio broadcasts can help intelligence analysts build up a picture of social and political developments within a country.

Public sources, like the news media, have also been a useful way of judging developments in the politics and government of the U.S.S.R. In the past, the May Day Parade in Moscow was the time when the U.S.S.R. rolled out its newest equipment, and while defense experts assessed the hardware, political and diplomatic experts looked at who was in prime position on Lenin's mausoleum. Over the years the rise and fall of players in the Soviet political scene could be judged by where they stood on the mausoleum to view the parade.

This form of intelligence gathering has its drawbacks, however, for not only can a cunning enemy manipulate it, it is also open to practical jokes. In the early 1960s *The Illustrated London News*, a long-standing and prestigious magazine, published a rather poor-quality photo-

ABOVE: A U.S. reconnaissance satellite with its solar panels deployed to gather energy to power its onboard sensors. Satellites can gather visual or electronic intelligence, and miniaturization has allowed more sensors to be fitted into a single vehicle.

LEFT: Iraqi radar stations destroyed by precision guided weapons during the 1991 Gulf War. With their radars and other sensors destroyed, the Iraqi antiaircraft ground defenses were in effect "blind," and Coalition aircraft penetrated the length and breadth of the country.

graph showing a Soviet fighter aircraft launching a powerful air-to-air missile. The publication announced that it had received the negative anonymously and thought that it had a scoop through a leak in the Soviet Air Force. Only later was it revealed that a talented aircraft model-maker had used the few existing photographs of the Soviet fighter to build a scale model. He had attached the model by fishing line to the clothesline in his back yard, and attached two simple firecracker rockets to the wings. The enterprising model-maker had then lit the touch paper on one and snapped a convincingly blurred low-angle photograph as it streaked away from the aircraft trailing smoke. The truth came out in *Flight*, a specialist aviation publication, which took more time analyzing the photograph and saw it as a fraud.

Published sources are also useful since they allow information acquired through clandestine sources to be given an open attribution. Your author recalls being shown four examples of the same map – one was secret, one confidential, one restricted, and one in the public domain. All showed the same information – the position of major units of the Group of Soviet Forces in Germany (GSFG). As the librarian explained: "If you are going

to publish something, make sure that your source is publicly available. You could be in trouble if the only source you can recall is one that is classified."

During the Cold War the means of gathering intelligence fell into 10 rough groups. There were overlaps between them; so, for example, information which seemed questionable, but which came from a usually reliable source, like a well-placed agent, might be confirmed through an entirely different source, like open literature.

An example was the report in a War-

TOP: Soviet rocket launchers on parade in Red Square on May Day, 1956. These parades gave the West an idea of current Soviet military developments, but were also a propaganda exercise.

ABOVE: Leonid Brezhnev, flanked by military and political leaders on Lenin's mausoleum, at the parade in 1976 commemorating the November Revolution.

saw Pact publication that the Czechs had developed a 152mm wheeled, self-propelled howitzer. There was no tradition within Soviet or Warsaw Pact ground forces for a wheeled artillery piece, and the information was viewed with some suspicion. It required a photograph and report by a defense attaché in Prague, who saw the 152mm SP Howitzer DANA at a parade in 1980, to confirm that a 152mm gun, probably based on the Soviet M-1973 (2S3), had been married to a turret and mounted on a Tatra 815 8x8 truck chassis.

This brought together two of the means of intelligence gathering – agents and open literature. The others are space imagery, aerial reconnaissance, ground observation, maritime observation, underwater sensors, electronic intercept, allied intelligence services, and defectors.

We discussed the role of space-based intelligence gathering a little earlier in the chapter. In essence, a reconnaissance satellite consists of the following elements: the camera and lens, film supply, a mirror which reflects the camera picture onto the film, a processor and dryer, a readout looper, video scanner, and the take-up and storage section. The photographs are taken as the satellite passes over target areas, and then, after processing, they are transmitted through a video TV link to earth.

The techniques which were developed to scan the surface of the moon and planets deeper in space can also be used to examine remote or hidden areas of the world. The Itek Pan camera uses a modernized version of the stereoscopic photography technique which transformed air photography and interpretation during World War II. The Itek Pan camera is a high-resolution panoramic camera which operates by rolling a strip of film across a rotating mirror which turns the image through 90 degrees and provides stereoscopic pairs by nodding back and forth.

The U.S. "Big Bird" satellite, backed up by the KH-11, replaced the reconnaissance satellites launched in the 1960s and 1970s. While the former gave a broad overview of areas, the latter provided detailed TV imagery of specific targets. The Big Bird could send both TV pictures and capsules containing film. As they floated down on a parachute, they could be recovered either by "Sky Snatch," which used a specially modified C-130, or

BELOW: An aerial reconnaissance photograph taken by the U.S. Air Force of the Soviet freighter *Kasimov* loaded with crated missiles on its way to Cuba. The Cuban Missile Crisis was precipitated by the Soviet move to place medium-range ballistic missiles on the island, within striking distance of the United States. Even after the crisis was defused in 1962, Soviet specialists remained on the island until the collapse of the Soviet Union in the 1990s.

if they landed in the sea, by "Sea Snatch." The Space Shuttle made the launch of reconnaissance satellites faster, cheaper, and more reliable, and allowed film to be recovered. Satellites also have a wide range of military uses beside reconnaissance and communications, and Global Positioning Systems (GPS) have transformed operations in remote areas.

Aerial reconnaissance dates back to the earliest days of flight. Balloons were used for observation in the American Civil War to give a version of what would be called "real-time intelligence" in today's intelligence language. It was in World War I that cameras were first taken into the sky, and since then aerial photography has been a constantly developing art. A number of factors come into play, including focal length and altitude – in essence, the higher the altitude the longer the focal length necessary to give a clear image. The forward motion of the aircraft means that an image would be blurred if conventional equipment was used – to overcome this, cameras are fitted with forward-motion compensation (FMC). This operates by moving the film by the exact amount needed to offset the image movement caused by the aircraft in flight.

Modern systems use microprocessors to control camera functions, shutter and aperture settings, the projection of digital data on the margin of the photograph, and also the FMC. The decision to use fast (sensitive) film or slow (less sensitive) and whether to use false color film to show artificially camouflaged objects,

LEFT: A McDonnell Douglas RF-4C Phantom II. The RF-4C is a multi-sensor reconnaissance aircraft equipped with forward-looking and oblique cameras, Infrared Linescan, SLAR (Sideways Looking Airborne Radar), and a small mapping radar.

BELOW LEFT: The camera from an AF Mirage 5BR reconnaissance aircraft. The quick turnaround of photographs following sorties is vital for tactical intelligence.

RIGHT: A pensive smile from Francis Gary Powers as he holds a model of the U-2 high-altitude reconnaissance aircraft. Powers was testifying to the Senate Armed Forces Committee in 1962.

BELOW: The wide wingspan of the U-2, which allowed it to fly out of range of most Soviet air-defense systems, shows clearly in this picture. U-2s were used to photograph military/industrial complexes deep inside the Soviet Union.

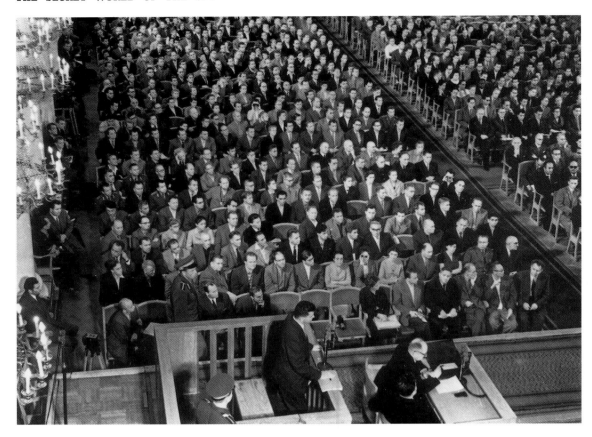

must also be taken. Finally, the pilot must choose whether to take vertical or oblique photographs. The solution to some of these questions is to mount several cameras – for example, in the nose and chin fairing of the venerable McDonnell Douglas RF-4C Phantom II there are three camera stations. These are usually one KS-72 or KS-87 forward-facing camera, one KA-56A low-altitude camera, and one KA-55A high-altitude panoramic camera.

Other airborne systems include Infra-red Linescan (IRLS) and Sideways Look-ing Airborne Radar (SLAR). Infrared detects the heat emitted from the target and so can be used by day or night. It is, however, more effective at night when ambient temperatures fall. Sideways Looking Airborne Radar allows a recon-naissance aircraft to fly along a hostile border and detect movement inside enemy territory. Advanced versions of SLAR technology are in use in Bosnia and were used in the Gulf War.

One aircraft of the many used for aerial reconnaissance deserves special men-tion. The Lockheed U-2 high-altitude re-connaissance aircraft operated over the U.S.S.R. between July 1956 and April 1960. The aircraft was the brainchild of the CIA, who hired pilots from the USAF to fly the aircraft into Warsaw Pact air space. It is said that 20 missions had been successfully undertaken before an air-craft flown by Francis Gary Powers was shot down by a missile near Sverdlovsk on May 1, 1960. Powers, an air force cap-tain, took off from Peshawar in Pakistan to fly across the U.S.S.R. to Norway. His aircraft was badly damaged, but he was able to parachute to safety – and a trial in Moscow. He was sentenced to three years in jail and seven in a labor camp. He served only two before being exchanged for the "illegal," Rudolph Abel. For Nik-ita Khrushchev the "U-2 incident" was excellent propaganda which he exploited at the Paris summit by way of making a dramatic exit.

Powers was subjected to a court of in-quiry when he returned to the United States, but no charges were brought against him. There were those in the CIA who felt that he should have pressed the destruct button on his aircraft before ejecting. There were reports, however, that some Chinese Nationalist pilots operating U-2s over Communist China, who had pressed the button after the engines "flamed out," had been destroyed with their aircraft. Powers may have decided not to risk it – however, when he was on the ground, he did not use the suicide pin containing shellfish toxin hid-den in a silver dollar. Despite these criti-cisms, in 1965 he was awarded the CIA's highest award, the Intelligence Star. He published his best-selling memoirs in 1970, but died in a helicopter crash in

1977 while working as a pilot for a Los Angeles TV station.

The aircraft type that Powers flew has enjoyed a long life. It was returned to production twice, once in the late 1960s and again in the 1970s. The final version in service in the early 1990s was the TR-1, which looks externally like the U-2R, but has improved electronic counter-measures (ECM) and synthetic-aperture radar system (SARS).

A second high-altitude reconnaissance aircraft, which is now mothballed, was the bizarre-looking SR-71 Blackbird. This was capable of a top speed of Mach 3, a range of nearly 3000 miles, and a maximum altitude of 86,000 feet.

Another aircraft design which has been invaluable in intelligence gathering and assessing, and which has therefore been widely copied, is the Boeing E-3A Sentry. By mounting a radar dish above the fuselage of the aircraft, which has a tactical radius of 1000 miles from base, Boeing and the USAF produced a system which proved its worth during the Gulf War. The Sentry has gone through

several versions since the E-3A first flew in 1977, and the concept has been copied with the Grumman E-2C Hawkeye, the Soviet Ilyushin "Mainstay," and the Tupolev Tu-126 "Moss."

Satellites and aircraft are the high-cost, and sometimes high-profile, areas of intelligence gathering. The intelligence gathered from them has, however, influenced the history of the postwar world. The presence of Soviet weapons and equipment, which precipitated the Cuban Missile Crisis of 1962, was only detected by air reconnaissance. Nearly 30 years later, King Fahd of Saudi Arabia allowed Coalition forces onto Saudi territory only after he had been shown satellite photographs of Iraqi forces massed close to the Saudi-Kuwaiti border, following the Iraqi invasion of Kuwait.

At the opposite end of complexity from aircraft and satellites is information gathered on the ground. This can be accomplished by simple observation, which may be by men in overt or covert observation posts. Your author has

BELOW: A Boeing E-3A "Sentry" Airborne Warning and Control System (AWACS) at Clark Base in the Philippines in January 1981. The AWACS has a flight crew of four; the rest of the crew of 12 to 15 is made up of specialists who are analyzing the data from the fuselage-mounted Westinghouse APY-1 radar.

visited Norwegian UN posts in south Lebanon and border posts above the Arctic Circle opposite the former Soviet Union. Both were very similar, fitted with radios and Japanese-designed high-powered marine binoculars. The men in the posts observed and logged the activities in the area visible from their posts. The U.S. Marines in Vietnam experimented successfully with marine binoculars linked to a laser rangefinder. If they detected a target, they could pass its range and bearing from their observation post to a fire base, and call down accurate fire on the target.

Hand-Held Thermal Imaging (HHTI) equipment, which was first used operationally by the British during the Falklands Campaign in 1982, allows observation to take place in day and night and also enables the soldier to see "through" external cover. Thermal imaging detects the small differences in ambient heat in both living and inert objects. Hot engines, and even warm faces and hands, can be detected. A vehicle behind a camouflage net or underbrush will show up as a warm mass visible through the

external cover. At a defense exhibition in the United Kingdom in the mid-1980s, this accuracy was shown to startling effect. A male and a female member of the Royal Military Police emerged from their office at the exhibition site and walked past a stand fitted with a closed-circuit TV TI camera. On the screen, their warm and cool areas showed clearly, but viewers could also see an image invisible to the naked eye – the clear, warm imprint of the man's hand on the woman's behind.

Two developments from the Vietnam War which have enjoyed considerable success are UGS and ADSID – UGS are Unattended Ground Sensors, and ADSID stands for Air-Delivered Seismic Intrusion Devices. With miniaturization both are now about the size of a can of baked beans, though the ADSIDs need some external protection since they are delivered from aircraft either in freefall or by parachute. UGS are emplaced by hand. Both devices can detect seismic, audible, or ferric signals, and in addition an infrared (IR) "gate" can be set up across defiles to provide an invisible barrier. When the

IR beam is broken, or men or vehicles trigger the seismic device, this information is transmitted by a tiny transmitter with an almost invisible antenna made of thin wire.

By positioning a booster station in the vicinity these signals can be passed to a remote command post for analysis. The devices can also be fitted with printers, so that they provide a permanent "hard-copy" record of movement in their area. Some systems are also designed to self-destruct when their battery life has come to an end. UGS have been used to cover remote border areas like those between Mexico and the United States or Northern Ireland and Eire, but on a smaller scale they can be used for ambushes and patrols. More permanent devices are low-light and conventional television monitors. These can be invaluable in anti-terrorist operations if sited near likely target areas, as they may record scenes before an incident takes place and so provide documentary evidence for arrests and convictions. Keyhole cameras can be fitted, to film or photograph through tiny apertures, and fiber optics allow the

LEFT: The USS *Liberty*, which was attacked by Israeli ships and aircraft at the beginning of the 1967 Six-Day War. The Israelis said that they had mistaken the ship for a hostile vessel; the reality is that they probably wanted to sink or neutralize it, so that the pre-emptive strike by the Israeli air force would not be detected by the sophisticated electronic warfare (EW) equipment aboard the USS *Liberty*.

RIGHT: A Soviet intelligence-gathering ship (right) with a minesweeper at anchor at the entrance to the Strait of Hormuz in 1987. Iran had warned ships not to enter the Strait during naval exercises by Iranian forces.

image to be transmitted over a distance.

Maritime intelligence gathering used to be important when Warsaw Pact and NATO fleets engaged in large naval exercises in the Atlantic. Electronic intelligence was used to build up a picture of naval operations and the frequencies of radars. Though since the end of the Cold War this type of operation has ceased, there is still a need for maritime surveillance to identify oil spillage, monitor the movement of ships through bottlenecks like the Strait of Dover, and, in areas of the Far East, to intercept pirate vessels that have been preying on shipping. A combination of fixed- and rotary-wing aircraft and ships, some of which are only small inshore patrol vessels, can be used to police and survey territorial waters. At the height of the Cold War, the U.S.S.R. operated about 40 "spy ships."

The U.S. Navy's experience with similar vessels was dogged with misfortune. In 1967 the USS *Liberty*, a 10,000 ton electronic-warfare ship operating off the Sinai Peninsula, which was monitoring Arab and Israeli radio transmissions in the days before the Six-Day War, was attacked by Israeli aircraft and ships which wrecked the electronic-warfare equipment and killed 34 of the crew and wounded 75. The Israelis claimed that they thought the *Liberty*, which was flying the Stars and Stripes, was an Egyptian ship, but it is unlikely that

Mossad would not have known its nationality and function. It can only be assumed that the Israelis did not want the United States to know about their pre-emptive air strikes against Egypt and Jordan, or their subsequent success.

In January 1968 the USS *Pueblo* was attacked while operating off the North Korean coast by a Korean warship. It was then boarded and captured. The crew was only released after Washington had admitted the ship's function and apologized. When the *Pueblo* was captured, the crew was unable to destroy documents and equipment.

Agents are not necessarily "cloak-and-dagger" operators working in hostile

ABOVE: Wounded crewmen from the *Liberty* aboard the carrier USS *America*. Initial casualty figures reported only four killed and 53 wounded, but this was revised upward to 34 killed and 75 wounded.

RIGHT: Released crewmen from the USS *Pueblo* board U.S. Army helicopters south of Panmunjom before being flown to a U.S. Army hospital on December 23, 1968. The crew were held for almost a year in North Korea when their ship was captured.

territory; they are also quiet, hard-working analysts whose accumulated experience and knowledge of the personalities, built up over years, can give unique insights into target organizations or communities. Those working in hostile territory may pass their information by radio: this will be either in burst-transmission or encoded form. In the Cold War the East German intelligence service used to pass messages to its many operators in the West in the same way as the Allies contacted agents in occupied Europe – over the international airwaves. Agents can pass information through personal contact, and though this can be dangerous for both parties, it can also be an opportunity for a case officer to build up background information over a drink.

An old and favored technique is the "dead-letter drop." The dead-letter drop, or mailbox, simply means that agents will leave written information or documents at a prearranged location for collection by their case officer. These places are usually relatively well hidden, and agent and officer may work out a simple code, like a chalk mark on a wall in the vicinity, to show if there is anything in the box. For added security, the information could also be concealed to look like refuse, or a common object like a stone or piece of wood. In an open society the mail can be used, and as the beginning of the chapter explained, the photocopier is a

fast and reliable tool for operators. If the mail is used, information can be concealed in microdots or even good, old-fashioned invisible ink.

Microfilm can be concealed in a vast number of ways and in some very unlikely locations. On one occasion during the height of the Cold War, a shopper in the United Kingdom bought a pair of shoes which had been made in Poland. When he returned home and laced them up, the tip of the lace came apart to reveal a piece of film which showed two men in conversation. The shoe importers were almost blasé about it and explained that

RIGHT: In the immediate postwar period there was an increased fear of Soviet spies in the United States. Here a reporter shows where a hollowed-out pumpkin was used as a dead-letter box for microfilm in December 1948.

ABOVE: Tracking transmitters produced in the 1980s – these would allow counterespionage or terrorist agents to follow suspects with transmitters planted on them, or would allow a lone agent to be tracked, if he or she was on a dangerous mission.

LEFT: Viacheslav Borovikov, the Soviet Embassy's security chief displays a two-foot-long pipe which was removed from a column in the embassy while it was being built in 1987. During the Cold War both sides bugged embassy buildings, sometimes using very sophisticated equipment, which was almost impossible to detect.

all sorts of odd things turned up in items imported from Eastern Europe.

In the past, Soviet and Warsaw Pact agents were able to operate much more easily in the open societies of the West than their NATO counterparts in Eastern Europe and the U.S.S.R. In the early 1990s, penetrating Islamic fundamentalist states, or the drug cartels linked by family and blood ties, is far harder and much more dangerous. Ironically, the erstwhile enemies of the Cold War have found common cause in combating these two threats.

As we observed in the previous chapter, a major source of information is electronic transmissions. Where operator's voices and idiosyncrasies can be identified, units can be traced as they are redeployed. At the Battle of Dien Bien Phu between March and May 1954, two French officers who had grown up in Brittany, aware that their radio transmissions were being monitored by French-speaking Vietminh soldiers, chose to communicate in their native tongue – Breton. It was entirely secure, since most Frenchmen find the language, which is similar to Welsh, completely baffling. However, when French operators in the HQ in Hanoi monitoring the radio traffic from the besieged fortified base heard this strange language on the air, there was considerable worry. It was logged as "an unknown oriental language," and

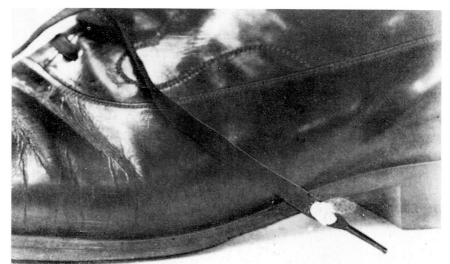

French military intelligence officers wondered if the Chinese had crossed the northern border with Vietnam to join in the fight, as they had in Korea.

At the other end of the scale from combat-radio nets are the tiny "bugs" that can be emplaced in buildings and equipment to transmit confidential conversations. Bugs can be placed inside a telephone to transmit either when the phone is in use or on the hook. They can be fitted inside such ordinary office items as a pen, cigarette lighter, or television. All the "bugged" objects will work convincingly as well as functioning as transmitters. The technology used in domestic baby alarms can also be employed for covert

ABOVE: Microfilm concealed in a shoe lace. Given its tiny size, and the amount of information that could be packed into it, microfilm was an ideal way of moving information discreetly.

RIGHT: In the summer of 1955 Bernard Spindel (left), an electronics expert, gave the Chairman of the House Judiciary Committee a startling demonstration of the effectiveness of "bugs" when he tapped the congressman's telephone. The photograph shows them examining the equipment, which by the standards of the 1990s are museum pieces, but which in the 1950s represented a frightening new area of surveillance.

BELOW: In a press conference in 1957 the Soviet authorities produced equipment which included radios, code books, and weapons. Public trials, the exposure of agents, and displaying their equipment was part of the war of nerves waged by both sides between 1945 and the late 1980s.

surveillance. Here the domestic electrical appliance is linked to a microphone and low-frequency transmitter, and at the far end a receiver and loudspeaker allow the conversation to be monitored.

Another technique is laser eavesdropping, which uses the glass in the window of a room to act as a modulator vibrating in sympathy with the speech of those inside, and so functioning like the diaphragm in a microphone – this can, of course, be defeated by drawing the curtains. In 1952 Soviet agents managed to emplace a bug 8 inches long with a 9-inch antenna inside the American eagle crest in the U.S. Embassy in Moscow. When it was discovered, the Americans exposed it in grand style in a meeting of the U.N. Security Council. Newer technology includes devices that can detect information being typed into a computer system by watching the pattern of key strikes on a typewriter. This allows a monitor to "see" the letter as it is being typed. Bugs may also be built into the fabric of a building, using the reinforced steel as an aid to transmission.

However, as Jamie Jameson explained at a conference in Washington, some electronic eavesdropping operations can backfire. The CIA had acquired the plans for a new building that was under construction, which they knew would be rented by the new chief of the KGB. Knowing that he would "sweep" the building for bugs, they made a calculated decision to target one room: it had only outside walls and one small window and was obviously the room he would choose for serious operational conversations.

"So," said Jameson, "they got a system that would make Harmon Karden envious of its stereo quality and built it in there so that nobody could ever discover [it]. We had hours and hours and hours worth of recorded Russian fairy tales, because they made that the nursery. All we got was the KGB colonel reading old Russian fairy tales to his children."

Eavesdropping on portable telephones was easy until recently, as scanners could be used to sweep the frequencies and pick up conversations. However, the same technology that was developed for

encrypted radios has been offered for commercial use. The system uses the natural spaces between the words in human speech. Each digitally coded conversation is chopped into short bursts and the coded bursts interleaved. The receiver stitches them together again. For an eavesdropper the only sound that can be heard is a continuous hiss. The current Clinton administration has endorsed a proposal by the National Security Agency (NSA) that the government be given the keys to allow them to monitor secure private communications by telephone, fax, or computer, since there is a fear that the system could be exploited by criminal or terrorist groups.

Another means of gathering intelligence is open source literature. As we saw at the beginning of the chapter, this can provide technical intelligence; it can also give an indication of future political or social moves. Official or semi-official newspapers or radio stations may include editorials and comment which have a subtext indicating the new government line. National leaders or foreign govern-

ABOVE: Viacheslav Borovikov at a press conference at the Soviet Embassy displays listening devices found at various Soviet establishments in the United States. Both sides built "secure rooms" constructed within the embassy using specially selected materials. In these rooms within rooms officials could discuss sensitive subjects.

ments may be praised or denigrated, or policies endorsed or condemned. The ability to read a foreign language and tease out all the nuances is essential in this type of work.

During the Falklands Campaign and the Gulf War, experts and pundits discussed the tactical options available to the British and Coalition forces, and while some former servicemen were very discreet and at pains not to "do the enemies' staff work," others came dangerously close to predicting the actual course of operations.

Sometimes governments may attempt to manipulate external as well as their own domestic media. A good example is the Iraqi government and the CNN tele-

vision channel during the Gulf War of 1990-91. Iraq tried to restrict TV crews from filming bombed bridges, but in one instance created a fake "baby-food factory" on the site of a bombed installation – this backfired because the baby-food factory was seen to be camouflaged and surrounded by barbed wire.

Allies can be a source of intelligence, though with the end of the Cold War there is no longer the unifying threat of the Soviet Union and Warsaw Pact to bond the allied nations of NATO in a common cause, and sometimes allied intelligence services may be operating in the same areas and competing rather than collaborating. In an ideal world the work load of intelligence gathering and

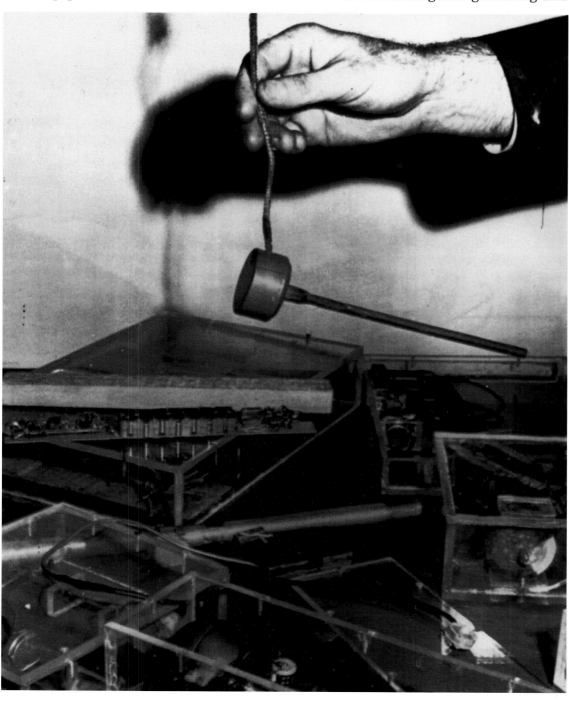

LEFT: In a press conference in Washington in May 1964, a State Department official shows one of more than 40 microphones found in the U.S. Embassy in Moscow when the walls were torn into in April. In the foreground are examples of listening devices found in U.S. Embassies behind the Iron Curtain. The device on display has a microphone and transmitter which are embedded with a long tube leading to the wall's surface. This presents a small surface area and is therefore harder to detect.

analysis can be shared. One unusual area where the British, United States, and French shared intelligence gathering was the missions in East Germany. These missions were a leftover from the end of World War II and were in theory liaison teams between the Allies (there were similar Soviet missions in West Germany). In reality they had become ways of gathering operational intelligence about new equipment and tactics.

NATO mission members were Russian speakers and traveled in high-performance sedans with special plates identifying them as mission vehicles. One veteran of these Cold War operations recalled that when the French were given the task of gathering information,

they were often rather lax and would explain that they had to take a long lunch break and so had been unable to finish the job. The U.S. mission could, however, often leave behind some rather jumpy and aggressive Soviet Army guards. This could be hard on the British, who were relatively discreet but would know when they found roadblocks and trigger-happy soldiers that the American mission had been through the area.

Allies can, however, be less than friendly, and the French external security service, the Direction General de Sécurité Extérieur (DGSE) has a rather checkered record: its most notable unfriendly encounter being the attack on the Greenpeace boat, the *Rainbow War-*

BELOW: A cigarette-case camera provided by the KGB for RAF Chief Technician Douglas Britten. In 1968 Britten was sentenced to 21 years in prison after he admitted to spying in Cyprus and the U.K. He was a radio technician who had access to valuable codes and equipment, and was trapped by the Soviets using a simple blackmail technique.

rior, in Auckland, New Zealand, on July 10, 1985. The boat was being used by anti-nuclear protesters, who were monitoring French tests on the Mururoa Atoll, when French agents attached a "limpet" mine to its hull. Following this attack the ship settled in the harbor and a photographer who went below to collect his equipment was drowned. Two DGSE agents were arrested on the island.

Of course, the most fruitful means of gathering information can often be defectors. Some may be from hostile intelligence organizations and can therefore expose their operations. Others may be artists, political dissidents, and intellectuals looking for greater freedom. They may have limited short-term intelligence value, but be able to give a "big picture" of life within their home country, which can be useful for political analysis. Defectors, however, can be unreliable. Sometimes they may wish to ingratiate themselves with their new hosts, trying to make their information fit into a pattern acceptable to them, or worse, they may be deliberately "placed" by hostile intelligence organizations. Hence, while there are numerous means to acquire intelligence, none are infallible, and the most reliable picture is usually the one built up from a variety of sources.

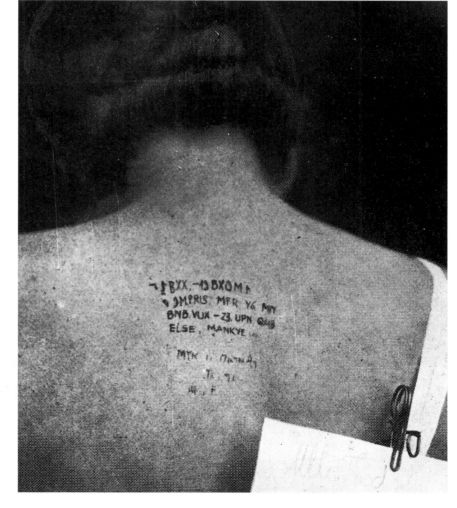

THE METHODS

The methods by which intelligence is gathered, collated, and analyzed vary according to the resources available and the nature of the information requirement. Thus a police/military counter-terrorist operation will rely on human intelligence gathered and collated into a computer database, while military operational intelligence will include information gathered from a variety of sensors, land-based, airborne, and even beneath the water or ground. The Falklands Campaign of 1982 and the Gulf War of 1990-91 showed that military intelligence-gathering operations in the field need not be against the old enemies of the Cold War. Indeed, in 1990-91 the Soviet Union provided some useful background information for the Coalition forces on Iraqi equipment and weapons. The threat of the future may well be from religious or nationalist groups funded by crime and waging a low-intensity terrorist campaign.

Whatever the nature of the conflict, each side will attempt to outsmart the other. In a frontline military context this can be as simple as avoiding unnecessary movement by men and vehicles, using camouflage nets, and covering headlights and mirrors on vehicles when they are parked to avoid sunlight reflecting off them. Vehicles and men may be sited behind cover in "dead ground," which conceals them from line-of-sight sensors like thermal imagers, image intensifiers, and radar. In a defensive position or concentration area, vehicles and men will move according to a track plan, which

conforms to a pattern similar to agricultural or commercial movement. Men and machines will be dispersed, and then hidden beneath trees and inside barns and large buildings – this not only makes them less of a target, but also makes them harder to locate.

Battlefield intelligence gathering – like its more sophisticated relations, technical, strategic, or political intelligence – can be systematic, but may also be reactive. A photo analyst, battalion intelligence officer, or signals expert may spot something that does not fit the normal pattern – extra vehicle movement, a prisoner of war from a unit not previously encountered in the area, an increase in the volume of signals traffic, or unexplained radio silence. These are all "signatures," which are a sign that something is about to happen. Thus, while camouflage and discipline may not defeat a determined enemy, they may prevent it from spotting a signature as he tries to collate and analyze the vast amount of information that may be coming in. If imagery from RPVs, satellites, or aircraft; the volume of signals traffic; or reports from reconnaissance patrols do not indicate anything unusual, the enemy will move on to study other tactical areas of responsibility (TAOR).

In the days of the Cold War, soldiers were taught to recognize signature vehicles and troops. These could be engineer AFVs and trucks, like bridge layers or mine-clearing vehicles. The ZSU-23-4 Shilka self-propelled AA gun indicated the presence of a regimental head-

RIGHT: At a snap VCP (Vehicle Checkpoint) in 1979 on a country road near Newry, Northern Ireland, a soldier of the Light Infantry covers the road. The war against terrorism includes overt operations like VCPs and patrols by the army in support of the police, and intelligence-gathering and covert operations. The end of the Soviet Union and Warsaw Pact has removed a source of weapons and training for terrorist groups, but racketeering is still used to collect funds to buy weapons and explosives.

Financial Empire of
Gonzalo RODRIGUEZ- Gacha

quarters, and certain types of armored personnel carriers could indicate whether the unit was tank- or infantry-heavy. Certain types of vehicle were recognizable as command posts (CPs) by their extra radio antennae, and these were priority targets. For men in a covert observation post, the order in which these special vehicles appeared moving down a road or axis of advance would give an indication of what the unit was and where the full weight of its fire power would be directed.

The demise of the Cold War may have reduced both the activities of the "great game" of espionage at a strategic level, and intelligence gathering at an operational or tactical level, but it has not removed the threat of terrorism or international drug-related criminality. Terrorists may no longer be backed by Eastern Bloc sponsor states, with training, equipment, and opportunities for rest and recuperation, but money laundering from drug profits and racketeering provide what one American analyst

called "M and M" – money and muscle. Hence Colombia and Peru are now prime targets for intelligence surveillance operations because of heavy drug trafficking; Syria and Libya are still seen as longtime sponsors of state terrorism; and Iran, Iraq, and North Korea, besides sponsoring terrorism, may also be nascent nuclear powers.

In the late 1980s the CIA was not involved with the drug war, today it has inserted agents into the Cali and Medellin cartels, and is training South American police in intelligence-gathering techniques. In February 1993 the CIA even began flying low-level air reconnaissance missions against the drug cartels. Its most successful operation was organizing the ambush in which the Colombian police killed Jose Gonzalo Rodriguez-Gacha.

Intelligence gathering in this new war comes in two forms: financial and operational. Financial intelligence is akin to the antiracketeering work undertaken against Al Capone in the Prohibition

ABOVE: In a press briefing in Washington in December 1989, Attorney General Dick Thornburgh uses graphic displays to show the size of the financial empire of Medellin drug-cartel leader Jose Gonzalo Rodriguez-Gacha, which totaled $61.8 million in banks in five countries. At the conference Thornburgh explained that authorities had frozen the accounts in Britain, Switzerland, Austria, Luxembourg, and the United States.

LEFT: Colombian police guard the bodies of Gonzalo Rodriguez-Gacha (front) and his bodyguards killed in a raid on December 16, 1989. The United States has provided training and technical assistance for the Columbian authorities in their war against the drug barons.

BELOW: Colombian troops prepare a two-ton cocaine haul for destruction at a farm in northern Antioquia Province on August 28, 1989. The equipment on the farm, which was owned by drug baron Jorge Luis Ochoa, was destroyed after the drugs had been burnt.

LEFT: Al Capone, the most widely known racketeer. His criminal empire created by blackmail, terror, and bribery was based on the illegal trade in liquor in the Prohibition years in the United States, and remains a classic model for study by police and intelligence officers. Many political terrorist groups use criminal methods akin to those of Capone to generate funds for their operations. In some cases the political cause is submerged in the criminal activities. Drugs are a major source of revenue, but protection rackets, which live off building and construction firms, or transport businesses, are also means of "making money." The willingness to use considerable force, either against people or property, to ensure that payments are made regularly is another distinguishing feature of these types of operations. Penetrating these criminal and politico-criminal organizations can be very difficult for security forces, since senior members may be linked by blood or marriage, or long service with "the cause."

ABOVE: The young J. Edgar Hoover, Director of the Federal Bureau of Investigation, in July 1935. The map in his office shows the agents in place in the United States. The numbered tags on the map show that the FBI was busiest in the big cities of the East and the Midwest.

years. Illegal sources of income from drinking clubs, gaming machines, construction scams, taxi firms, and, of course, straightforward bank robberies must be traced back. It is harder where these businesses deal almost exclusively in cash, as the illegal operator can simply spread his or her hands and say, "Well that was a good month and the other one was not so good," to explain the apparent lack of income in his books.

On an operational front, police and soldiers must be able to identify the color and license plates of suspect cars, as well as the drivers and passengers, though terrorists can also use public transport or simply walk to the target they wish to attack. Closed-circuit television (CCTV) has made security easier and has also

allowed video film to be studied after an event – in some cases, however, the videotape has not been installed and so unique opportunities to examine the terrorist at work have been lost.

In a world before CCTV, during the Algerian War, four French Army parachute regiments moved into Algiers in January 1957 to take over police functions and found that intelligence files on FLN (National Liberation Front) terrorists were completely inadequate. The FLN had launched a series of attacks against the French and Algerian-born, French-speaking colonists. In turn the colonists had bombed the Casbah, a warren of narrow streets in the old Arab quarter of Algiers. The police could no longer combat this terror, and the paras were brought in from the mountains, where they had been fighting rural semi-regular FLN units, to fight an urban guerrilla war.

As part of their tactics, they divided the Casbah into numbered blocks and then subdivided it down to individual houses. Algerian-Arab residents were appointed to be responsible for blocks and houses, and a night-time curfew was imposed. This meant that the paras of the 3rd Colonial Parachute Regiment could conduct raids on houses, and if an individual was either not at home or was in the "wrong" house, they were an immediate suspect. Suspects could be held overnight for questioning, and if they "broke" under interrogation to reveal names or hiding places, then there was a rush to arrest more suspects before the dawn came, which would allow the FLN to move more freely and assess the damage to their organization.

The FLN had adopted a classic cell structure in which members would only know or meet two or three subordinates and would in turn report to one superior. This meant that the organization was

RIGHT: French soldiers man a cordon around buildings in Algiers during search operations against the FLN (National Liberation Front), in May 1956. These men are probably reservists called up for duty in Algeria — the more demanding operations were conducted by paratroopers, marines, and legionnaires.

BELOW: *Pieds Noirs*, Algerian-born Frenchmen, break through a police cordon during protests in December 1956 over planned reforms for the then French colony of Algeria. *Pieds Noirs* and French Army attempts to keep Algeria French, after de Gaulle had agreed to independence, produced the OAS (Secret Army Organization), a right-wing terrorist group that waged war against the government in metropolitan France and Algeria.

hard to penetrate, though sometimes by good luck or tactics the para intelligence officers would unravel a cell structure. Such discovery would usually result in the death or arrest of the FLN cell's members. Using these tactics, the paras won "The Battle of Algiers," but at the cost of liberal public opinion in France and Western Europe, since they earned themselves a reputation for brutality in the process.

The police are usually seen as the main force for combating terrorism, since they are closer to the community and generally have better intelligence and contacts. As a member of the Ulster Defence Regiment (now amalgamated with the Royal Irish Rangers to become the Royal Irish Regiment) explained: "If I am on a VCP (Vehicle Checkpoint) and I look at a driving license and ask the driver where he is going, I will know if he

LEFT: A soldier of the 3rd Battalion The Light Infantry guards a constable of the Royal Ulster Constabulary as they check details of a commercial vehicle near Fermanagh, Northern Ireland. The registration of the vehicle and its owner's name can be checked in minutes by a radio message to a central computer.

BELOW: A soldier in Londonderry checks the identity of a man in a Republican area of the city in January 1992. Vehicle and personnel checks may produce intelligence, but they may also antagonize the local population and must be conducted with politeness and tact.

is taking a long route from his home, whereas a regular soldier over on a tour from the mainland will not know the local geography as well." Police and paramilitary forces may be closer to the community, but this can make them vulnerable to intimidation and corruption. The sums of money involved in drug dealing can be vast, and a policeman or border patrolman may be offered many times his yearly salary merely not to patrol a stretch of road at a certain time or to come on duty slightly late.

If a crime is committed and then followed up by the police and security forces, it is harder to gain a conviction in some cases because terrorists have become more adept at protecting themselves from forensic examination. By using one-piece overalls and wearing surgical gloves they reduce the chance of the police detecting the presence of minute traces of burnt powder from ammunition on their clothes or hands. In addition, there will be no fingerprints on weapons, or on the wrapping for explosives. However, there have been cases when a quick follow-up by the police and security forces has found a suspect in the shower at home removing any final vestiges of powder from his body.

Lawyers who defend individuals who are involved in terrorist activities may by design or accident discover details of police forensic or detection procedures, and in turn the terrorists will work out ways of circumventing them. Cars can be stolen moments before an attack, which means that if a soldier or policeman checks the registration it comes up as "neutral." The only way around this is to compare the name of the driver's license with that registered as the owner – this can be done very quickly by a radio linked to a computer, but is only effective if a VCP is in position.

At observation posts and checkpoints soldiers and police are constantly on the lookout for wanted individuals. However, terrorists are adept at changing their appearance, as were Soviet "illegals" operating during the Cold War. Simple changes in hairstyle, clothing and makeup all help to change appearances radically. When Ernesto "Che" Guevara entered Bolivia in 1967, he cut off his striking long hair and beard, donned spectacles, and shaved his head to escape notice. Soldiers and policemen have learned to recognize shapes which are harder to alter, like chin, nose, eyes, and ears – but even here cosmetic sur-

gery can be employed. Key members of a terrorist organization can be kept off the streets. Leaders, planners, bomb makers, and quartermasters (who store weapons and explosives) can be shadowy characters who may be spoken of, but rarely seen, and are therefore hard to keep track of or arrest.

Such a figure was the leader of the Peruvian Maoist organization, the Shining Path, or Sendero Luminoso – an organization which took its name from a quotation by the founder of the Peruvian Communist party who said in the late 1920s, "Marxism-Leninism will open the shining path that will lead to the revolution." Known as Gonzalo, the leader of the Shining Path, Abimael Guzman Reynoso was arrested on September 12, 1992 following a painstaking police and counterterrorist operation. He was living in an upper-story apartment in a quiet suburb of Lima. His organization, which had combined Maoist Marxism with drug dealing, had been responsible for the deaths of over 25,000 people.

The operation which led to his capture had used information about his health, eating, and smoking habits, and the fact that a slim young dancer, who was meant to be living alone in the apartment, had

been buying considerable amounts of food for her apparent sole consumption. The area was staked out by male and female agents, some of whom pretended to be street cleaners, while others acted as if they were courting couples. After they had built up a clear picture of the apartment, an elite counterterrorist group assaulted the building and captured "Gonzalo." In a scene which might have been written in a novel, the head of the Peruvian antiterrorist force confronted Guzman soon after his arrest. The Maoist academic was remarkably calm and said coolly to his captor, "Sometimes you win and sometimes you lose." "This time you lose," was his captor's reply. As a shrewd psychological ploy the shadowy leader was put on show in his striped prison uniform, and the public had the opportunity to see that "the fourth sword of Marxism" was in fact a fat, bearded, and bespectacled, though still dangerous, man.

The successful capture of Guzman had been a major priority for President Alberto Fujimori of Peru, and as part of his campaign the president conducted a "gentle coup" and disbanded the parliament to rule by decree. It was popular with Peruvians, who saw their congress-

ABOVE: These youthful male and female members of the Maoist organization, the Shining Path (or Sendero Luminoso) are aged between 12 and 27. They are posing for this photograph in the Andes 375 miles southeast of the Peruvian capital Lima. Often very young terrorists are the most dangerous, since they may have grown away from their parents and being unmarried have no close family for whom they feel responsible. They can be manipulated by older members of the group and used for dangerous and dramatic terrorist missions.

RIGHT: Abimael Guzman (57) who was known as Chairman Gonzalo when he headed the Sendero Luminoso. A ruthless and shadowy figure, his capture was a major coup for the government of President Fujimori. He was captured by a combination of excellent intelligence work and quick action by counter-terrorist teams. Subsequently the Peruvian government put Guzman on show at a press conference on September 24, 1992, in a calculated psychological move to demythologize him. The fat, bearded, and bespectacled man, as prisoner 1509, was still aggressive and charismatic behind bars, but it marked a major triumph in the war with the Shining Path.

men as not only corrupt, but also ineffective against the Shining Path. The United States, however, saw the move as undemocratic and therefore cut off military aid. On April 24, 1992, this move had lethal results for the crew of a U.S. Air Force C-130H surveillance aircraft.

In May 1993 *Newsweek* reported that the aircraft, with a crew of 14, took off from a base in Panama on an operation codenamed "Furtive Bear" to overfly the coca fields in Peru. President Fujimori, angered at the ending of U.S. aid and the continued intrusions into Peruvian air space, ordered the Peruvian Air Force to intercept suspicious aircraft. Two Soviet-built Su-22 fighters were scrambled to intercept and force down the C-130H. The U.S. Air Force crew was told by its controllers in Panama to ignore the fighters. The fighters opened fire with cannon; the aircraft decompressed, and Sergeant

LEFT: Flanked by Minister of Defense, Victor Malce (left) and the Minister of the Joint Armed Forces, Nicolas Hermoza, President Alberto Fujimori attends a military parade in March 1992. Fujimori's "coup," in which he disbanded the government and ruled by decree as a way of combating terrorism and rebuilding the economy, was popular with the country which saw its politicians as corrupt.

BELOW: A Peruvian policeman in the ruins of a police station destroyed by the Shining Path. The terrorist organization used car-bomb attacks and individual assassinations as a way of enforcing its will on society. Its funding did not come from the former Eastern Bloc, but from drug and protection rackets.

Joseph Beard Jr. was sucked out and fell to his death. Eventually the C-130H made an emergency landing, whereupon it was surrounded by Peruvian soldiers. Peru insisted that its fighters thought that they were engaging a drug-smuggling aircraft. *Newsweek* says that a secret U.S. Embassy cable states that the pilots knew they were shooting at an American aircraft since they were close enough to make eye contact. "Whatever the truth," says the magazine, "both sides eventually decided to keep the real story to themselves."

Often gun or bomb attacks by terrorist

Weapons have varied from handguns, to automatic weapons like the AKM (a later version of the AK-47, a 7.62mm assault rifle), to belt- or magazine-fed light machine guns which are used in rural areas. While a handgun is easy to conceal, the weight of fire from an assault rifle can be sufficient to outshoot a normal police patrolman.

Explosives can be stolen from quarries or construction sites, or may have been acquired from Czechoslovakia in the days of the Cold War. Known generically as Semtex, this explosive takes its name from the explosives factory at Semtin

or drug cartels are conducted by less sophisticated "foot soldiers," who receive their weapons and equipment from quartermasters who hold them in secret hiding places. If the attack involves using a handgun, the terrorist will be able to dispose of it quickly after the event to an accomplice, who in turn passes it back to the quartermaster. In this way if the terrorist has been recognized he will be "clean" if arrested.

and comes in several types. The Semtex that has been used for terrorist attacks is Semtex H, which was first produced in 1967. In response to demands from the international community that Semtex should be made easier to detect, the Czechs have finally incorporated marking agents into Semtex so that it can be detected more easily by explosives "sniffers." Semtex is a powerful high explosive, and has a detonating velocity

ABOVE: The bus in which eight British soldiers were killed and 28 injured when the IRA exploded a roadside bomb on August 20, 1988. The soldiers had been returning from leave and were on their way to their base at Omagh, Northern Ireland.

of 7650 yards per second. This is similar to most modern plastic explosives, which all have a shattering effect on an urban environment. Semtex can easily cut steel members in a bridge or building.

An explosive that is easier to make and is widely used by terrorist organizations, is based on ammonium nitrate fertilizer into which is mixed diesel oil or sugar. The "homemade" explosive requires a booster charge made from a plastic explosive, like Semtex H, to be effective. These homemade explosives have a lower detonating velocity – about 4900 yards per second – but they create a slow-moving shock wave that can be devastating in built-up areas. Because this type of explosive is bulky, it is normally delivered to its target in a car or truck.

A tactic developed by terrorists during some of the longer campaigns, which is similar to one employed by the Soviet KGB and East German HVA, is to use individuals who have apparently never undertaken any subversive acts in their lives. These people have steady jobs in the community but are called "sleepers"

LEFT: Scottish police remove the body of a passenger killed when the Boeing 747 on Pan Am flight 103 was destroyed by a bomb over Lockerbie, Scotland, on December 22, 1988. Controversy still surrounds the incident, with Libya being blamed for the attack which has been seen as an act of "state-sponsored terrorism." Two Libyan intelligence officers have been named as the men who placed the explosive device in the baggage, and U.N. sanctions were enforced against Libya in an attempt to have them brought to trial, but allegations of Syrian, Iranian, and even U.S. culpability continue to surface.

BELOW LEFT: A young commuter reads the *Evening Standard* at a London station in 1992. IRA bomb attacks against the British capital have targeted restaurants, transportation, the commercial center, and military forces on public duties. Though IRA ASUs (Active Service Units) can conceal themselves in the city, it is a harder environment in which to work compared to the towns and cities of Northern Ireland.

RIGHT: Broken windows in the Hong Kong and Shanghai Bank building, which was damaged by an IRA car bomb on April 11, 1992. The attack killed two people and injured 80. It also produced huge demands on insurance companies, as well as disrupting the work of the City, London's financial center. The IRA had learned that an attack in London produced a far greater propaganda return than one in Northern Ireland.

in counter-terrorist and espionage jargon, since they are ready to be "awakened" when they are needed for a mission or task. They may simply be asked to provide a vehicle, store weapons or explosives, or hide an active cell that is on the run from the security services.

Chance arrests by checkpoints or based on observation do still happen, but intelligence has moved increasingly toward using informers who penetrate organizations to provide intelligence. This type of work calls for patience and an ability to build up a special type of relationship. When a New York Police team and FBI men raided an Islamic fundamentalist bomb factory, mixing ammonium nitrate-based explosives in a garage in the suburb of Queens in July 1993, they were acting on information provided by an Egyptian, Emad Salem. Known as the "Colonel," he was a

LEFT: Emergency vehicles surround the twin towers of the World Trade Center in New York, following the Islamic terrorist bomb attack on February 26, 1993. The blast killed five and injured 300. For the United States it was an ugly reminder of the world of terrorism, which seemed to be confined to Europe and the Middle East. By a combination of good detective work, and ineptitude on the part of the terrorists, the World Trade Center bombers, and another group which was allegedly planning attacks in New York, were arrested before they could cause further death and damage.

ABOVE RIGHT: A workman looks through a hole in the floor of the World Trade Center following the attack. The terrorists used simple explosives which can be manufactured from fertilizer, and which, though bulky and not as powerful as commercial or military explosives, are still very effective when detonated in a confined space, like the underground parking lot at the Center.

43-year-old former officer in the Egyptian Army and part of the inner circle around the blind, fiery Egyptian cleric Sheik Omar Abdel Rahman. Salem became an informant partly for cash (he was paid $250,000), but also because he thought that terrorist killings would further betray the cause of Islam. The terrorists had planned to attack, among other targets, the Holland Tunnel between New York and New Jersey with a 500-pound bomb. Though this would not have breached the walls of the tunnel, it could have created an underground fire, killing many drivers through smoke inhalation and oxygen starvation as well as blast or crushing injuries. Fortunately this plan was foiled, but the destructive capability of this alarmingly simple explosive was amply demonstrated in the World Trade Center bombing.

Clearly the "Colonel" saved many lives, but is now himself at risk. Using informants inside an organization can be a risky business both for the "handler," who is the informant's point of contact, and, of course, for the individual who decides to talk. The decision to inform is usually made for one of two reasons. Informants may decide to betray their friends because they have become disenchanted with an organization or its methods, or they may be blackmailed into working with the police or security forces.

In the first instance "turned" terrorists can be as deadly to their former comrades as they were to the security forces, since they have so much valuable information to offer. During the fighting in Oman in the early 1970s, the Communist-led rebels known as *Adoo* (or enemy) who crossed over and joined the Sultan's forces were led by British Special Air Service (SAS) officers and NCOs in groups known as *firquats*. They were not only

ABOVE: Nidal Ayyad is led away from the Federal Court at Newark, NJ, after being denied bail on March 12, 1993 following charges of aiding and abetting the World Trade Center attack.

RIGHT: Flames and smoke obscure the front of the American Embassy in Beirut following an attack on April 18, 1983. The attack in the early hours of the morning collapsed the front of the seven-story building located on the seaside corniche of west Beirut. The U.S. diplomatic and military presence abroad had always been a target for terrorist attacks, notably in Germany and the Middle East. Like their British counterparts, U.S. servicemen and civilians were urged to dress down and conduct themselves in a way that did not attract attention and so make them obvious targets. Patterns of behavior, like strict time-keeping or fixed routes to or from work, had to be modified so that terrorist groups could not set up an ambush to kill or kidnap them.

invaluable for their local intelligence but also for their skills as natural warriors. The SAS argued reasonably that a man who is fighting for you is far better than a corpse or a PoW.

An informant who is blackmailed into working for the security forces may be arrested for a minor offense and then confronted by the police with the fact that they know more about their personal or family background. To protect them-selves, or those close to them, from arrest and more serious charges, it is often easier to cooperate as an informer. Once caught up in the business of being a double agent, the informer is in a difficult situation that he cannot escape from. He could be arrested by his security force handlers, or murdered by his terrorist comrades. For handlers, getting to know an informant and building a relationship can be quite difficult, for on a personal

basis they may find the idea of an individual who betrays their trusted friends and comrades extremely distasteful. However, they must work with the informant, who in turn may see the handler as the only real friend they have. Interestingly, women often make better handlers than men, and the CIA is now making greater efforts to recruit them.

If informants have has been compromised and are in danger of being murdered by the terrorists, the security forces have the financial resources to allow them to leave the country and begin a new life. While anonymity and a large amount of cash may seem like a recipe for a safe escape, it is often hard for relatively unsophisticated people to make the break from a close-knit family or regional group, and sometimes they return to visit, occasionally with fatal consequences. An added problem is that, in order to retain a degree of credibility with the subversive organization, the informer must participate in criminal or terrorist acts, or at least be an accessory to them. This gives the security forces the dilemma of knowing that a criminal act will be undertaken, while also knowing that they will compromise their informer if they act to prevent it. If the terrorist act is, for example, a bank raid, handlers and their higher controllers may be able to accept this as the price for gaining deeper knowledge of the organization and its members, which will in time lead to arrests and sentences. If, however, the informer knows that a murder has been planned, then the problem for the security forces is very serious.

If informants are exposed by the terrorist organization, they can expect no mercy. Normally after a brutal interrogation they will be shot and their body

dumped somewhere where the security forces will find it; it may even have improvised explosive charges fixed to it, or emplaced nearby, to kill or injure police or soldiers. Sometimes victims are dressed in "sterile" clothing, like one-piece overalls which will give the police little in the way of forensic information. A grimmer alternative adopted in some drug-related criminal murders is to remove the head and hands of the victim, which makes identification much harder. Thus in both drug trafficking or terrorist-related activities there are none of the gentlemanly arrests, trials, sentences, and quiet exchanges for double agents or informants that used to occur in the Cold War days.

The world of espionage and counter-espionage between East and West may have diminished with the warming of the Cold War and the breakup of the Soviet Union, but threats to society of a dif-

LEFT: The U.S. Ambassador to Bonn, Richard Burt, points to his car as he accompanies the Soviet dissident Anatoly Scharansky across the Glienicke Bridge in Berlin following an exchange with a Soviet agent on February 11, 1986. The world of "spy swaps" ended with the end of the Cold War and the destruction of the Iron Curtain. Though espionage continues, it is aimed more at economic intelligence, and this can often be gained by research, rather than by "spying."

ferent nature have developed. With borders more porous and groups and individuals more mobile by land, sea, or air, terrorism and sophisticated international criminal activity have become the new menaces. They may be fired by nationalism, religious fundamentalism, drug dealing, or, for the "foot soldiers," the simple thrill of power that comes from the barrel of a gun or an explosive charge. This presents the intelligence

and security forces of the world with a new challenge. Some, like the CIA, have found that formerly cooperative allies, now see them as intrusive, since these formerly friendly organizations feel that with the end of the Cold War there is no major threat. In the ultimate irony, some intelligence services have started to monitor the activities of their allies who are engaged in the war against terrorism and international crime.

ABOVE: Berliners celebrate the New Year in 1990 in front of the Brandenburg Gate three months after the destruction of the Berlin Wall. The wall has gone and Germany is united, but the economic and human cost has been high.

THE MYTHS

Factual accounts and histories of espionage are like a walk along the seashore. They contain a truth which can be as unpleasant as the flotsam and jetsam washed up along the coast, but there can also be some real treasures among this refuse. The real characters that inhabit this world range from the exotic and brave to the sad, unpleasant, and anonymous; while some are simply contemptible. But there are many agents who have entered espionage with motives of patriotism and their actions have inspired many writers and film makers.

Two women who became involved in intelligence work in World War II for the highest of motives became the subjects of films in the 1950s. In 1950 Anna Neagle played Odette Churchill in *Odette*, a film about an Anglo-French woman who operated in France, was captured and tortured, but who survived to be awarded the George Cross. Eight years later Virginia McKenna played the role of Violette Szabo, who operated in the Dordogne and was captured after a shoot-out in 1944. She was executed at Ravensbrück on January 26, 1945.

Not far from this grim seashore of reality are the polluted inshore waters of fact and fiction known as "faction." Authors, writers, and film makers who work these strange waters have, through contacts or research, built up a good background knowledge, and either to protect their sources or to spin a better yarn, use the medium of fiction. The attraction of their work is that the reader or viewer knows that its source is accurate. Some writers have said that the reality is so bleak, they use fiction to make it easier on their public.

Many of these works do not divide the world into the "good" West and "bad" East. Politics, corruption, and the career interests of senior players in the secret services blur the distinctions of good and bad, as innocent men and women are sacrificed in the interests of international politics or big business. The unquestioned twentieth-century master of this genre is John Le Carré; other well-known writers include Ian Fleming, John Buchan, Frederick Forsyth, Len Deighton, Graham Greene, Eric Ambler, Tom Clancy, and Martin Cruz, and many of these have seen their books turned into excellent films.

Spy thrillers and plays have a long and interesting history. Some were written with the intention of alerting the public to the threat of foreign military expansion and penetration by spies, others simply to tell a good story. Joseph Conrad's novel, *The Secret Agent*, which was written before World War I, portrayed a group of East European anarchists planning an attack on the Greenwich Observatory in London. Conrad drew the inspiration for his book from a true incident in which an anarchist had been blown up by his own bomb close to the Greenwich Observatory.

As alliances changed at the beginning of the twentieth century, the "enemy" for the British switched from France to Imperial Germany, and many of the alliances predicted by these writers

RIGHT: Roger Moore as James Bond, the British agent 007 — the double zero prefix indicating that he is "licensed to kill." Ian Fleming's character, with its mixture of British *sang-froid* and bravura style, became a popular book and film cult hero, with audiences entranced by the gadgets and throwaway one-liners (even if the plots could be a little lightweight).

LEFT: John Le Carré photographed in June 1989 at the time of the publication of *The Russia House*, which reflected the end of the Cold War and the changes in the Soviet Union under Mikhail Gorbachev. Le Carré's novels had a grim feel of authenticity about them, with their mixture of operations and office politics. In retrospect, he felt that the way he had portrayed the intelligence services as efficient had preserved a false myth.

became reality in World War I. The factual writers in this field include Chapman Pincher, John Barron, E. H. Cookridge, Richard Deacon and Nigel West.

Recently, John Le Carré, who published *The Night Manager* in July 1993, gave an interview to *Time* magazine at his home in Cornwall, England. He had some trenchant views on the intelligence business. As both a writer and a former intelligence officer, Le Carré re-

marked that he felt that espionage had been counterproductive in helping to preserve national security. "Where I kick myself is where I think I actually contributed to the myth of the intelligence services as being very good. When I wrote *The Spy Who Came in from the Cold*, the head of operations at the Secret Intelligence Service remarked that he was the only bloody double agent that ever worked. The mythmaking that went on all around us contributed to the kind of ingrown and corrosive self-perceptions that were the heart of our undoing."

Interestingly, the film version of *The Spy Who Came in from the Cold*, produced in 1965 and starring Richard Burton, was very well received by the critics and the public. Burton played an agent intent on getting even with his East German counterpart. The film had an excellent supporting cast and was shot in black and white in some grim urban landscapes.

If Le Carré's view of the world of espionage is bleak, it is understandable given his early experience. He explains that "if you live in secrecy, you think in secrecy. It is the very nature of the life you lead as an intelligence officer in a secret room that the ordinary winds of common sense don't blow through it. You are constantly looking to relate to your enemy in intellectual, adversarial, and conspiratorial terms. It is absolutely necessary to the intelligence mentality that you put your worst interpretation upon your adversary."

Such an adversary disappeared with the reunification of Germany. One of the major players in this secret war, who was the model for fictional East German spymasters, was the handsome, six-foot-tall head of the Hauptverwaltung Aufklärung (HVA), the intelligence arm of the

BELOW: Richard Burton and Claire Bloom in the film of Le Carré's *The Spy Who Came in from the Cold*. Produced in 1965 in black and white, the film had a grimy seediness which gave it a grim authenticity. Le Carré joked bitterly that the head of operations in the British Secret Intelligence Service claimed the hero of the story to be "the only bloody double agent that ever worked."

Stasi, Lieutenant General Markus Johannes Wolf. Wolf's organization was able to penetrate the whole of West German society, even placing Günther Guillaume, a HVA agent, as West German chancellor Willy Brandt's chief aide. At its height, the HVA had an estimated 6000 agents in West Germany, and even as late as July 1993 a spokesman for the Office for the Protection of the Constitution (BfV), Germany's domestic intelli-

gence service, revealed, "We assume that there are still some 300 valuable agents who have not been uncovered."

Wolf was a career intelligence officer, trained in the U.S.S.R., whose first mission had been to attend the Nuremberg war trials for the KGB as a journalist under the name of Michael Storm. A good organizer and leader, he sent congratulatory telegrams to HVA operators on occasions like birthdays and wedding

ABOVE: Elegant, professional, and very effective, the tall, bespectacled former head of the East German intelligence services, Markus Wolf, arrives with his wife Andrea and lawyers Johann Schwenn and Wolf Roemig at a Düsseldorf court in 1993. Wolf was given a six-year sentence.

anniversaries. Wolf made a break with the convention of using men as agents and not only sent female HVA operators into West Germany, but also sent HVA men to woo older women working as senior secretaries and personal assistants in military, industrial, and political posts. The agents "encountered" these women at bus stops and in cafeterias. One secretary testified that she photographed documents from a West German politician's office, then smuggled the film into East Berlin, attaching it to the underside of a toilet seat in a train.

In July 1993, Wolf appeared in court in Düsseldorf charged with treason and bribery. Wolf's defense was an interesting legal challenge: he had been a hard-working and loyal servant of the East German government for 33 years, so how could he be charged with treason? "I do not dispute the fact that I headed my country's intelligence service, nor that I met with the agents who worked for it. What government am I supposed to have betrayed?"

The real problem for the Germans was that Wolf was very good at his job, while the West German BfV had failed in theirs. There are reports that, although Brandt had been warned that Guillaume was a security threat as early as 1973, he remained in the Chancellor's office for another year. Indeed, in the year when suspicions were growing, President Nixon had the U.S. Ambassador in Oslo hand deliver a sensitive letter to Brandt, who was on holiday in Norway. It detailed the tensions between the members of the Western Alliance over nuclear defense and was a very sensitive document. Brandt passed it to his chief aide, Günther Guillaume, who sent copies to Bonn, and to his real boss, General Wolf.

During the court case in Düsseldorf, both Wolf and Guillaume, one as defendant and the other as witness, said that they had not wished to harm Brandt, whose conciliatory policy toward the Communist East they admired and respected. Wolf pointed out that he was still in a unique position to undermine the

LEFT: The West German chancellor Willy Brandt (left) with his close aide Günther Guillaume in Munich in 1972. Brandt resigned in 1974 when it was revealed that Guillaume was an East German agent. Though Guillaume passed on highly confidential material to the East, he liked and respected Brandt, who was making efforts to build bridges between East and West.

LEFT: Greta Garbo in the 1932 film *Mata Hari*, the first of three films about the ill-fated Dutch woman. Subsequent versions were *Mata Hari, Agent H.21*, a French film starring Jeanne Moreau (1964), and the 1984 film *Mata Hari*, which had Sylvia Kristel in the title role. Critics are unanimous that Garbo's version is the finest.

German government, given the amount of information he still had access to. However, in December 1993 Wolf was found guilty and sentenced to six years in prison.

HVA spies working in West Germany were often ruthless. Speaking in court, an agent known as Roland Gandt said that he had posed as a Danish journalist and seduced a young West German woman who worked as a NATO translator. The two became engaged, and Gandt persuaded her to spy for East Germany, but the woman, a devout Roman Catholic, became consumed by guilt. Gandt took the woman to Copenhagen to visit her future mother-in-law, an HVA agent, and brought her to a Catholic church, where her confession was heard by a priest – another HVA agent. Absolved, she felt free to continue spying.

Stories like this were useful material for writers like Len Deighton. Deighton, who has over 20 books to his credit, 18 of which are thrillers, served in the Royal Air Force as a photographer attached to the Special Investigation Branch (SIB). A detailed knowledge of Germany and spoken German equipped him to write about the espionage intrigues of the Cold War, and several of his books were made into films. The protagonist in the three best-remembered espionage movies, *The Ipcress File*, *Funeral in Berlin*, and *Billion-Dollar Brain*, was played by Michael Caine. Deighton had never given this character a name in the books, but, like

the author, he was from the north of England. The film's scriptwriters called him Harry Palmer, and Caine, reflecting his working-class origins in London, gave him a cockney accent.

The Ipcress File, produced in 1965 by Sidney J. Furie, has been described as the best of Caine's performances as Harry Palmer. The complex plot involves a missing scientist, an enigmatic piece of recording tape, electronic brainwashing, and top-level treachery. *Funeral in Berlin* has a plot which thickens "almost to the point of congealing," with everybody tailing everybody as Palmer is dispatched to Berlin to get the real story after a Soviet intelligence colonel, the chief of security on the Wall, has been reported as being anxious to defect. The interesting feature of *Billon-Dollar Brain* is that the villain is not a Soviet agent, but a Fascist Texan general called Midwinter, played by Ed Begley, who plans to invade the U.S.S.R. with the aid of a computer and his own private army. In the excellent supporting cast Oscar

Homolka plays the Soviet general who collaborates with Palmer to prevent the war.

One Berliner who tried to combine life and art was Hans Joachim Geyer, a spy-thriller writer who, in the late 1940s and early 1950s, under the pen-name Henry Troll, wrote paperback novels. In 1951 he volunteered to work for the West German intelligence organization run by General Reinhard Gehlen. This later became the Federal Intelligence Service, or Bundesnachrichtendienst (BND), but which was known as *Das Org* (the agency) by its staff. Geyer was sent to East Berlin to find prospective agents. Here he was approached by operators from the East German security service who turned him with blackmail and bribery. He then proceeded to supply them with the names of West German agents. Geyer enjoyed his role and began chasing women. This proved to be his downfall, when he boasted about his job to a girl who thought that his shadowy work was something to do with trading in prostitutes. She told her cousin, who was a

LEFT: Humphrey Bogart, Ingrid Bergman, Claude Rains, and Paul Henreid in *Casablanca*, which was first screened over 50 years ago and still captivates audiences. Though strictly more of a thriller than a spy film, *Casablanca* uses the uncertain world of neutrality in war as its basis. Neutrals, like Switzerland and Sweden, were important in World War II for intelligence services since they could provide a haven for agents on the run, or a place to deliver information.

detective, and he called at Geyer's home, announcing his rank to the housekeeper. This terrified the author, who fled to East Berlin. At a press conference in the East, he exaggerated his importance, attacked Gehlen, whom he called "a Fascist lackey of dollar imperialism," and even managed to put a plug in for his new book, *At the Beginning Was the End*.

An intriguing trilogy of spy plays was written by the British actor and playwright Alan Bennett. His first, *The Old Country*, starred Alec Guinness as an elderly former civil servant living with his wife in the country. As the play develops, the audience begin to realize that they are exiles. A visitor to the couple ex-

plains that the character played by Alec Guinness is to be exchanged, though phrases like "spy swap" are never used. It is never entirely clear whether the inspiration for the Guinness figure is Kim Philby – Bennett said that W. H. Auden, living as an artistic exile in the United States, was his model.

The British actress Coral Brown saw the play, and over dinner with Bennett and Guinness, told them of a visit she made to Moscow on tour with the Old Vic theater company in 1958. She was contacted by Guy Burgess and, visiting him in his small and untidy apartment, had a long conversation with him. Bennett used these incidents in *An Englishman*

LEFT: Cary Grant with Ingrid Bergman and Claude Rains in the 1946 film *Notorious*. The film, set in South America during World War II, had special agent Cary Grant blackmailing the alcoholic Bergman into providing sexual favors for the German Rains as a way of getting information. It was less of a war thriller than a film about a cruel love affair.

ABOVE: Frank Sinatra and Janet Leigh in the 1962 film *The Manchurian Candidate*. The film has Laurence Harvey as the brain-washed former GI from Korea with a mission to kill. Screened a year before the assassination of President Kennedy, the film was uncannily prophetic. The cast includes James Gregory as a ranting McCarthyite Senator, and Angela Lansbury as his politically ambitious wife and mother of Harvey.

LEFT: Julie Andrews and Paul Newman in the 1966 film *Torn Curtain*. Newman plays a defecting scientist who is followed to East Berlin by his fiancée/assistant (Andrews), unaware that he is playing a double-agent game. Like *Notorious*, the film is about trust and betrayal, with Andrews doubting Newman's loyalty to her and the American way.

Abroad, a TV play which subsequently transferred to the stage. The original starred Coral Brown, playing herself, and included incidents she had described, like the theft of soap by Burgess and his drinking habits, as well as a request that she order some new suits to be made by his tailor in London.

Finally, after Anthony Blunt had been exposed, Bennett wrote *A Private View*. This play included an intriguing piece of fiction, in which for the first time on stage Queen Elizabeth II was portrayed as a fictional character. The underlying theme in *A Private View* was the juxtaposition of perception and reality. The use of X-ray photographs, which are also used in artistic restoration, to show a hidden deeper image, was an ingenious metaphor for Blunt's respectable public role as the Keeper of the Queen's Paintings and his secret role as a spy.

Frederick Forsyth, who worked as an overseas correspondent for British newspapers, turned his hand to political thrillers, with *The Day of the Jackal*. Drawing on the background of the real assassina-

tion attempts against President de Gaulle following the French withdrawal from Algeria, its plot hung on the idea of the OAS hiring a professional assassin to kill de Gaulle. Forsyth's novel was successfully made into a film in 1973. It starred Edward Fox as the anonymous assassin codenamed "The Jackal," pitted against the ruthless bureaucracy of "democratic" France in which torture and phone tapping by the security services are seen as routine.

Michael Caine found himself back in a middle-aged Harry Palmer-type role in the film version of Forsyth's novel *The Fourth Protocol*. He attempts to foil a plot by rogue KGB "illegal" agents operating overseas without the sanction of any official Soviet organization. The villan is a distinctly flashy Soviet agent, played by Pierce Brosnan, who rents a house close to a USAF air base in East Anglia in England. He then builds a battlefield nuclear weapon, which his KGB bosses intend him to detonate to destabilize Anglo-American cooperation.

A USAF air base in Britain is also

ABOVE: Edward Fox, "The Jackal," is checked, along with other blond foreigners, at the Menton customs office on the French-Italian border. Based on Frederick Forsyth's novel *The Day of the Jackal* (1973), the film was about an assassination attempt on President de Gaulle, with Fox as a hired killer employed by the OAS. Fox is particularly sinister with his polished minor-public-school style, sportscars, and cravats, and he has no qualms about killing in order to cover his tracks as he moves toward his goal.

ABOVE: A gun-wielding secret serviceman scans the rain-swept streets of New York following a killing in the 1940 film *Foreign Correspondent*. The film starred Joel McCrea, Laraine Day, and Herbert Marshall, and had McCrea and Day searching out Nazi agents in the Netherlands and London following the disappearance of a peace-seeking diplomat.

LEFT: *Foreign Correspondent* (1940) anticipated later films in the way that ordinary objects became sinister or threatening. A camera conceals an assassin's gun, the sails of a windmill conceal a sinister secret, and the sanctuary of Westminster Cathedral provides an opportunity for murder.

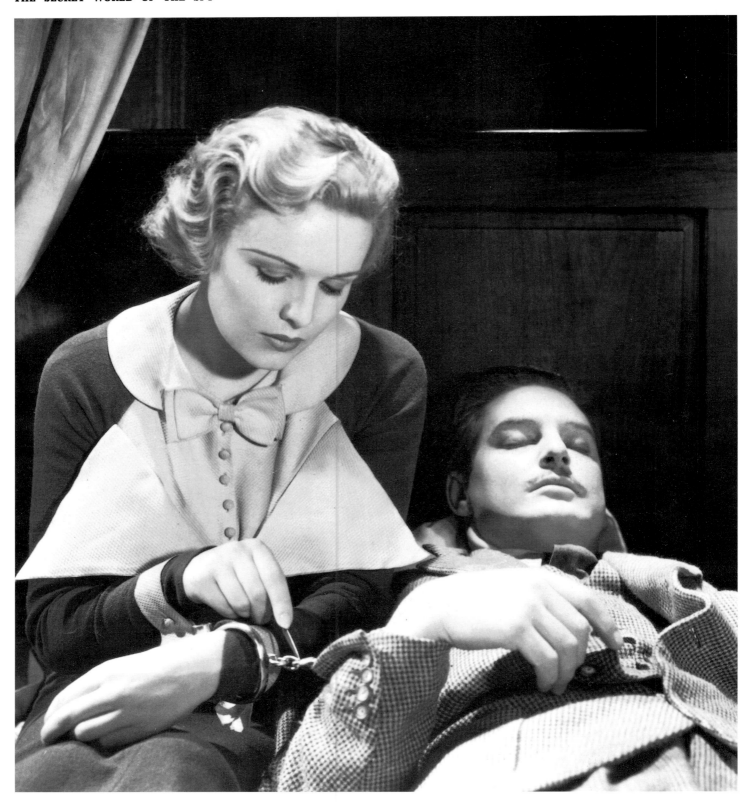

significant in an interesting film made in 1985. *Defence of the Realm*, which starred Gabriel Byrne, Greta Saatchi, the late Denholm Elliot, Ian Bannen, Fulton Mackay, and Bill Paterson, has Denholm Elliot as a far-from-crusading hack journalist who senses a greater mystery behind a political scandal. The "enemy" in this film is not the U.S.S.R., but the British and American Establishment hiding the death of a young man during a

nuclear accident at a USAF base. They are protected from public scrutiny by the Defence of the Realm Act.

British television ran a high-budget thriller series called *Edge of Darkness* in which actor Bob Peck played a policeman attempting to untangle the background to his daughter's death. She had been involved with a group of ecology activists investigating an underground former nuclear-weapons site which had been

ABOVE: The 1935 version of *The Thirty-Nine Steps*, starring Robert Donat, Madeleine Carrol, and Godfrey Tearle was the first of three films of the book by John Buchan. The film captures the confusion and fear of the hero, Richard Hannay, as he finds himself a fugitive in his own country.

bought by an international corporation. Peck finds that his enemies are big business and, eventually, elements of the British government and intelligence services. The idea that "friendly" intelligence services may, through mistaken identity, or for their own reasons, wish to pursue an innocent man or woman is a recurring theme in the spy thriller, and one of the best examples is John Buchan's novel *The Thirty-Nine Steps*.

Terrorism in films and books falls into a slightly different category from espionage; however, many of the organizations set up to counter espionage have been redeployed to counter terrorism. Thus books and films like *The Crying Game*, *Patriot Games*, and *Little Drummer Girl* use terrorist groups as the new enemy. In a post-Cold War world, terrorism and drug cartels are not only a real threat, but give book and film scriptwriters new

ABOVE: Madeleine Carrol and Robert Donat on the run from the British police and a German spy ring in another scene from the 1935 version of *The Thirty-Nine Steps*.

ABOVE: Harrison Ford and Anne Archer in *Patriot Games*, based on the thriller by Tom Clancy. Ford plays a CIA man drawn into the Northern Ireland conflict when he rescues a member of the British royal family from an assassination attempt.

RIGHT: Diane Keaton in the 1984 film, *The Little Drummer Girl*. Based on John Le Carré's novel, it has Keaton as an actress recruited by Mossad to track down a top Palestinian terrorist.

LEFT: Forrest Whittaker, as a British soldier kidnapped by the IRA, faces his last moments as Stephen Rea is ordered to kill him in *The Crying Game* (1992). The film won an Oscar in 1993.

material. Thus the latest James Bond film no longer has the agent fighting SMERSH or the KGB, but in mortal combat with South American drug barons.

Finally, there are the far seas of pure fiction, and here Ian Fleming's James Bond stands supreme. It is a world of beautiful women, menacing (but often slightly ludicrous) villains, car, aircraft, or speedboat chases, gunfights, daring escapes from impossibly tight corners,

and throwaway one-liners. The reader or viewer abandons rationality and escapes into a world in which he or she knows that the hero will come out alive, even as the villain is supervising a slow and terrible death. Reality in these circumstances would be a *mokrie dela* (wet job) — two rounds to the head and two to the body, if the enemy were the KGB or GRU. Mossad has a similar reputation and is generally regarded as having been

LEFT: Dusko Popov was said to be the model for Fleming's James Bond. The playboy agent passed valuable information to the Allies in World War II. He died aged 70 at his home in southern France on August 24, 1981. Commenting on the Bond character, Popov said that he would not have survived if he had behaved like the fictional agent.

RIGHT: Roger Moore in the 1981 Bond film *For Your Eyes Only*. The pose with the Walther PPK pistol was first adopted by Sean Connery and became one of the trademarks of the film Bond, as, of course, did the abundance of beautiful (but expendable) women.

responsible for the death of the Canadian ballistics expert and designer of the Iraqi "Super Gun," Dr. Gerard Bull. Bull was found shot dead in a Brussels suburb on March 22, 1990 – his wallet still containing a large amount of U.S. currency.

Interestingly, Fleming's creation was not a creature of pure fiction. There was a very real basis for his fantasy figure. Dusko Popov, the son of a wealthy Yugoslav family, was not only a daring and

highly competent spy but also had a taste for beautiful women, and was reported to be the model for Bond. While the fictional Bond has fought various enemies, including the KGB and drug cartels, as well as sinister megalomaniacs, Popov was a spy for the Allies in World War II. Popov, though he hated the Germans, had convinced them that he was a friend. He was able to pass to them information doctored by the British Secret Intelligence Service and in turn gather information from the Axis. Code-named "Tricycle," he became part of the Double XX system run by Sir John Masterman, who specialized in turning German agents and using them to plant false information.

Among Popov's coups were the unmasking of "Cicero," a German agent working as a valet in the British Embassy in Ankara, and giving early warning of the development of the V-1 flying bomb. Popov also gave the Americans indications that the Japanese planned to attack Pearl Harbor. However, J. Edgar Hoover expressed distrust and disapproval of Popov and his lifestyle. Popov's code name "Tricycle," Hoover suggested, indicated that "he had

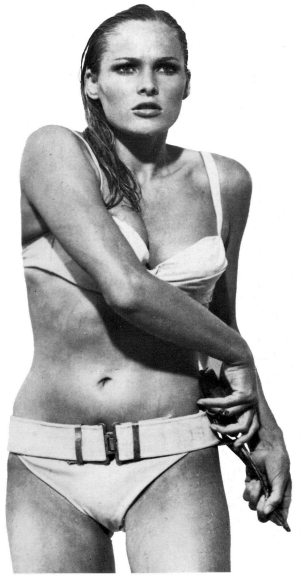

a liking for bedding two girls at a time."

The first Bond was played by Sean Connery, and although the role has subsequently featured several different actors, notably Roger Moore, the handsome Scot will always be the "real" Bond for many. *Dr. No* was the first film to be made from the Ian Fleming novels, in 1962, and it set the style for subsequent Bond films. There was a gleeful blend of sex, violence, and wit, and looking back one realizes

LEFT: *From Russia with Love* (1963) was the second Bond film and arguably the best. It has Connery as Bond and Daniela Bianchi as the Russian agent, who is remarkably vivacious compared to the plastic dollies later Bonds toyed with.

BELOW FAR LEFT: Ursula Andress, as Honeychile, appears from the sea in *Dr. No* (1962), the first Bond film. *Dr. No* had some notable scenes, including Bond's encounter with a tarantula and Dr. No's assault course of pain.

BELOW LEFT: *Goldfinger* (1964) has Gert Frobe planning an uncomfortable end for Bond (Connery) as a laser beam cuts its way toward our hero. The film had some classic touches, including the opening, in which Bond emerges from the sea under a bobbing sea gull attached to his scuba gear and strips it off to reveal an impeccable white tuxedo.

RIGHT: Sean Connery was a relatively unknown Scottish actor from a working-class background. He had done jobs like french polishing and delivering milk in Glasgow before he landed the role of Bond. It was said that Ian Fleming was initially unhappy with the casting, but Connery's skill as an actor shaped the character into a folk hero.

the extent to which the later films got bigger but not better. Eventually all the novels were turned into films and when this stock had been exhausted, new Bond scripts were written.

Just as Michael Caine escaped from being typecast in Harry Palmer roles, so too did Sean Connery, and both men went on to enjoy long and successful careers in acting. Connery played the part of the Soviet submarine captain in the film of *The Hunt for Red October*. A Russian officer with the United Nations watching a video of the film commented, "Yes he speaks Russian – but with a strange accent." Connery never entirely lost his Glasgow accent.

Whereas the Bond portrayed by Moore was altogether more frivolous, as well as sexually promiscuous and rather morally ambivalent, the Bond played by Timothy Dalton in *The Living Daylights* was a

"new man," with a genuine romantic engagement making him more of a Buchanite hero. The precredits for the film had Dalton as Bond making a free-fall parachute landing on Gibraltar in an exercise with the SAS to test its security. The film was produced in 1987, and on March 6, 1988, fiction and reality collided when, in an undercover operation, the SAS ambushed and shot dead three IRA terrorists who were planning a car-bomb attack on the band of the Royal Anglian Regiment.

If most of the Bond films were a pastiche of genuine espionage and counterespionage operations, *Casino Royale*, produced in 1967 and starring David Niven, was a clumsy attempt to send up the genre. It had Bond called out of retirement to do battle with SMERSH. For Fleming, SMERSH was a useful enemy for Bond and his masters, and in fact it did exist: its title was the acronym of the Russian phrase *Smert Shpionam* (Death to Spies). Set up by Stalin in the late summer of 1942, it was divided into five administrations: No. 1 worked in the armed forces and its job was to root out treachery and defeatism; No. 2 was responsible for collecting information and dropping agents behind the enemy lines; No. 3 collated and distributed information and orders; No. 4 was the investigation branch whose members had powers of arrest; and No. 5 was composed of tribunals which heard cases and passed sentence (there was no appeal against the sentences, and the death sentence was by summary execution).

Having completed its sanguinary business, SMERSH was wound up in 1946 and eventually became incorporated into the KGB (Komitet Gosudarstvennoi Bezopastnosti). In four years it had killed thousands of men and women. Little was known about SMERSH in the West until 1972, when a former officer, who had defected, published *Nights Are Longest There*. The author, Boris Bakhlanov, was at pains to conceal his identity, and the book was published under the name Romanov, while Bakhlanov had changed his name to Hatton. In 1984 Hatton/Bakhlanov was found dead, drowned in a pond on Wimbledon Common in London. A coroner returned an open verdict on his death. Had SMERSH claimed its last victim?

Fleming, who had worked in intelligence in World War II, used his knowledge to add other touches, which gave the early Bond books a certain authenticity. Whereas Bond reports to "M," the real head of the Secret Intelligence Service (SIS), or MI6, has long been known as "C." This dates back to the days of

Captain Sir Mansfield Cumming, RN, who, in 1911, set up an organization to counter foreign spy systems. Cumming left a permanent mark on MI6, which he controlled until he retired in 1929. His officers were gentlemen, though he had time for men like Sydney Reilly, "the Ace of Spies," who penetrated Bolshevik Russia. Another of his officers was Compton Mackenzie, the writer and novelist, who worked for the service in Athens and was fined after being prosecuted under the British Official Secrets Act when he later wrote about his experiences.

Another feature of the Bond films was the fantastic gadgetry developed by "Q." Though some of these were designed to protect our hero or assist him in escapes, others were lethal. Here too fiction and reality again coincide. The Special Assistant for Scientific Matters at the Central Intelligence Agency, Dr. Sidney Gottlieb, lived in a former slave's cabin on a 15-acre estate near Washington, where he grew Christmas trees for sale and kept goats, which provided his wife and four children with fresh milk. Despite having a clubfoot, his hobby was country dancing. He had a Ph.D. in chemistry and was also an expert on poisons.

In September 1960 Dr. Gottlieb received instructions from Richard Bissel, the head of the CIA's "dirty-tricks department," to arrange poisons to kill an African leader, who turned out to be Patrice Lumumba, the President of the Congo (now Zaïre). Gottlieb set to work with staff from the "Health Alteration Committee" and, with assistance from the U.S. Army Chemical Corps, produced a packet of likely poisons, which were sent to Africa by diplomatic pouch. Gottlieb himself assembled his equipment, including syringes, surgical gloves, and masks, and set off for the Congo to contact the CIA station chief.

Here the men plotted ways of administering the poison, but with insufficient information about Lumumba's lifestyle, they were unable to finalize a scheme before the poisons began to deteriorate. They were thrown into the Congo River and Gottlieb returned to the United States. There is no record of what effect they had on the river's wildlife.

Asked by members of the Church Committee on alleged assassination plots why he had participated in this work, Gottlieb explained why he chose to fight in the "silent war" that was being waged. "I felt that a decision had been made at the highest level that this be done, and that as unpleasant a responsibility as it was, it was my responsibility to carry out my part of it."

This work included an attempt to kill Iraqi leader General Kassem with a poisoned handkerchief, and Fidel Castro with poisoned Havana cigars, a poisoned wet suit, and even an exploding conch shell placed to attract his attention while scuba diving. There was one fatality from this work: Dr. Frank Olsen, who threw himself from a tenth-story window at the Statler Hotel in New York while under the influence of drugs. He had been taking part in an experiment with mood-

RIGHT: Flanked by bodyguards, the young Fidel Castro addresses the crowds during the march on Havana on January 24, 1959. If the U.S. government had not seen Castro as a Communist threat when he took power in Cuba and had established a working relationship with him, they could have neutralized a threat to the stability of Central America and the Caribbean. In the early 1960s the CIA looked at ways of assassinating Castro, which included poisoned cigars, explosive charges, and even a poisonous scuba wet suit.

LEFT: Robert Vaughan and David McCallum in one of the film versions of the 1960s TV series *The Man from UNCLE*. Both film and TV versions used a formula based in part on the Bond series and also on the cops-and-robbers two-man team. Interestingly McCallum played Ilya Kuryakin, a Soviet member of UNCLE — the United Nations organization dedicated to combating terrorism.

RIGHT: A dapper Robert Vaughan with the heavily modified P38 pistol, which was one of the trademarks of *The Man from UNCLE* series, in the computer room of the UNCLE headquarters.

altering drugs and had ingested LSD. Following this death, Richard Helms, head of the CIA, ordered Dr. Gottlieb to cease work and destroy the records as the agency came under investigation following the Watergate scandal.

Other tools developed by the CIA included photographic, communications, audio surveillance, surreptitious entry, incendiary, and explosive equipment. Probably the most bizarre was the radio transmitter T-1151tv/USG Straight Stitch Peat Moss, better known as the "Dog Doo" transmitter. This was a radio homing device about four inches long, with a range of several miles, which could be used for target designation for attack aircraft. It resembled "the excrement of a dog, or other similar animal."

Agents could be equipped with lock-picking tools and even makeup kits with false mustaches and beards. For escape

RIGHT: *Mission Impossible* — another TV series which dressed its cast in neatly tailored suits or elegant dresses and then asked them to accept missions against international criminal organizations.

and evasion they could carry a four-inch-long, one-inch-diameter suppository which contained: (a) one pair of wire cutters, screwdriver, pry bar, and tool handle (in combination); (b) two pointed saw blades; (c) two flat saw blades; (d) one drill; (e) one reamer; (f) one flat file, and (g) one ceramic blade. Developed in 1962, it was designated "Suppository, E & E Mark 1." Instructions stated, "The kit is generally carried in a pocket or briefcase and should be concealed rectally, as circumstances require."

The KGB had its own range of tools and equipment, and launched its own assassination operations against targets in the West. One of its operatives was Bogdan Stashinsky, a young, good-looking Ukrainian who had been pressed into service with the KGB in the early 1950s after he had been arrested for traveling on a train without a ticket. He began work as a courier and agent in West Germany. He was good at his job, and at the age of 25 was promoted to an assassination squad, which conducted its operations using chemical weapons.

His first target was Lev Rebet, a fellow Ukrainian living in Munich. The weapon used on Rebet was a gun fired by a percussion cap which ruptured an ampoule of prussic acid vapor. The acid vapor emerged as a spray and then produced symptoms akin to a heart attack in its victim. Stashinsky was briefed that the vapor would not affect him as long as he took prophylactic medication before and after the attack. As a test run, and to prove that the equipment worked, his masters instructed him to experiment with a dog in the woods in East Berlin. In 1957 he met Rebet on a stairwell leading to his Munich office and the subsequent autopsy pronounced that the Ukrainian

had indeed died of a heart attack. Stashinsky's next mission was to kill Stephan Bandera, another Ukrainian exile living in Munich. Stashinsky stalled the KGB but, under pressure, he again used the chemical gun and killed Bandera. The KGB was delighted, awarded him and promised promotion.

At this point, almost like a movie plot, the female lead appears. Stashinsky met and married a sensible East German girl called Inge who, when she heard about his "work," persuaded him to escape to the West. He crossed into West Berlin and surrendered to the Americans. At his trial in West Germany, he gave a detailed confession and managed to pre-

LEFT: Jack Lemmon and Sissy Spacek in *Missing* (1982) – a film based on the true story of an American writer who "disappeared" during Pinochet's coup d'état in Chile in 1973. Lemmon, as the man's father, and Spacek, as his wife, attempt to discover his fate from the U.S. and Chilean authorities.

sent himself as a victim manipulated by the KGB. As a result he received a sentence of only eight years as an accomplice to murder. The West gave the case considerable publicity, and consequently the KGB was forced to reconsider its policy on assassination and employ it only in exceptional cases.

The CIA developed a number of assassination weapons, including the single-shot 9mm pistol, better known as the

"Deer Gun." It was a simple weapon which was intended for potential resistance organizations in Eastern Europe — the philosophy behind its design was that it would be used to kill a soldier at close range, which would allow the resistance worker to take the soldier's rifle. The Stinger .22in. Reloadable was a weapon similar in concept, but very compact. A .22in. single-shot weapon was even produced disguised as a cigarette. A rod pen-

ABOVE: Robert Redford, in *Three Days of the Condor* (1975), starred opposite Faye Dunaway in a world of CIA power games, scientific hardware, and a Borges-style riddle: why should a mystery thriller that didn't sell be translated into obscure languages?

cil which resembled a drafting pencil, but which instead of a lead contained a sharp steel spike, was produced for use as both an offensive and defensive weapon. Silenced weapons included the Walther pistol and the Springfield .30in. M1903 rifle. The silent bio-inoculator fired an 0.8-inch-long dart tipped with M-99 tranquilizer: the dart gun was intended for silencing guard dogs. Dogs could also be silenced using tranquilizer capsules or

"puppy chow," which rendered them unconscious for four hours. If, following an operation, a CIA agent wanted to revive the dog, a syrette of antidote was included in the kit.

A German-born agent whose operational lifestyle approached that of a Bond figure was Wolfgang Lotz. Nicknamed "the Champagne Spy," he was the child of a German father and Jewish mother who escaped from Germany

before World War II and settled in Israel. Lotz joined the British Army and worked in intelligence, interrogating PoWs from the Afrika Korps in North Africa. He joined the Haganah, the Israeli underground force, after the war, and was promoted to major in the newly created Israeli Army. Mossad realized that a man who could pass himself off as a German veteran of the Afrika Korps was a useful asset, and they were able to send him to Egypt, where he posed as a German of independent means. Breeding horses at a stud farm and mixing easily with Egyptian society, he gave valuable insights into the thinking of Egyptian military and political leaders. One of his operations involved the sending of letter bombs to former Nazi scientists who were working on missile programs in Nasser's Egypt. This had the desired effect, and the Germans returned home.

The Egyptian German missile program features as part of the plot of Frederick Forsyth's *Odessa File*, which has a young German journalist (played by John Voight) track down the former SS officer (Maximilian Schell) who killed his father. The SS man is now the director of a major electronics company which is supplying technology for the Egyptian missiles. Mossad assists the reporter in tracking down and killing the former SS man. The title of the book and film comes from the organization that smuggled wanted former Nazis out of Europe to Latin America.

Having succeeded in disrupting the missile program, Lotz continued work for the Israelis but was arrested when Egyptian radio-detection vehicles located his hidden transmitter. In 1965 he and his German wife, Waltraud, were tried and found guilty of spying. Lotz managed to keep up

ABOVE: *La Femme Nikita* (1981) is a French film which was subsequently made into an English-language version. The intelligence services use Nikita, a girl with drug problems, and therefore expendable, as their hitwoman.

his German façade and so avoided the death penalty, but he was nevertheless sentenced to life imprisonment.

Following the Israeli success in the Six Day War of 1967, he was one of the prisoners that the Israelis demanded in exchange for 500 Egyptian officers captured in the fighting. Ironically, the good life he had enjoyed ended with his release. Financial loss and personal bereavement left him as an elderly man working in a Munich department store, scraping by on his $200 Mossad pension. Perhaps Bond would have ended in similar obscure retirement if film makers and scriptwriters had not granted the character eternal youth.

Film and book reviewers may have predicted that the end of the Cold War marked the end of the spy thriller as a genre, much as the western was said to be dead. However, just as real intelligence agencies will point to terrorism, drug cartels, and unstable nations with nuclear or chemical capabilities as a justification for their continued existence, so too scriptwriters, film makers, authors, and publishers will continue to find material in these areas.

BELOW: *No Way Out* (1986), starring Kevin Costner, Gene Hackman, and Sean Young in an update of John Farrow's 1947 film *The Big Clock*. The film confirmed Costner as a star in the role of an officer called in to investigate the murder of the mistress of a devious U.S. Secretary of Defense played by Hackman.

INDEX

Page numbers in *italics* refer to illustrations

Abdel Rahman, Sheik Omar 89
Abel, Col. Rudolph Ivanovich, *1*, 58
aerial reconnaissance *55*, *56*, 58, 59
agents 6, 10-33, 55, 62, 64
  "legals," "illegals" 39, 48, 58
  recruitment requirements 13, 16
  "sleepers" 29, 86-7
  vetting, screening 16-17, 19
  vulnerable areas for 19-23, 25-6, 27, 29, 31, 32
Air Delivered Seismic Intrusion Devices (ADSID) 61
aircraft, American,
  AV-8B Harrier *41*
  Black Hawk helicopter *39*
  C-130 55, 83, 85
  E-2C Hawkeye 59, *60*
  E-3A Sentry 59, *59*
  RF-4C Phantom IV *56*, 58
  SR-71 Blackbird *2-3*, 59, *60*
  Stealth aircraft (B-2, F-117) 51
  U-2 (TR-1) *2-3*, *8*, 20, *57*, 59
  V-22 Osprey 51, *51*
aircraft, British, Vulcan 41
aircraft, French, AF Mirage 5BR *56*
aircraft, Soviet 40, 54, 59, 83
Aldridge, Lance Corporal Phillip L. 25-6
Algeria 77-9, *78-9*
Ambler, Eric 94
Ames, Aldrich 26
André, Major John 32, *33*
Andress, Ursula *112*, *114*
Andrews, Julie *103*
Ansary, Rafaat el- 22-3
Arab-Israeli war 62, 125
Archer, Anne *109*
Argentina 38, 41
Arnold, Benedict 32, *33*
assassination equipment 116, 118-21
atomic-bomb spies 7, *11*, 29, 45-6
Auden, W. H. 102
Ayyad, Nidal 89

Bakhlanov, Boris 114
Ballistic Missile Early Warning System (BMEWS) *40*
Bandera, Stephan 120
Barron, John 96
battlefield intelligence gathering 72, 74

Beard, Sgt. Joseph, Jr. (USAF) 85
Begley, Ed 101
Belozerov, Dr. Arkadu 49, 50
Benn, Anthony Wedgwood *17*
Bennett, Alan 102, 104
Bergman, Ingrid *101*, *102*
Berlin 34, 39-40, *92-3*
Besidin, T. A. 50
Bianchi, Daniela *112*
Bingham, Sub-Lt. David (RN) 10, 12, *13*
Bingham, Maureen 12
Billion Dollar Brain, novel and film 100, 101
Bissel, Richard 116
blackmail 17, 19, 20
Bletchley Park, England *42*
Bloom, Claire 97
Blunt, Anthony 29, 31, *31*, 104
Bogart, Humphrey *101*
"Bond, James" character 109, 110, 112-13, 114, 124
Bornholm, Denmark 39
Borovikov, Viacheslav *64*, *68*
Bosnian conflict 58
Bossard, Frank 26-7
Bourdine, Vladimir 27
Boyle, Andrew 29
Brandt, Chancellor Willy 98, 99, *99*
Branegan, Jay 51
Brezhnev, Leonid *54*
Britten, Chief Technician Douglas (RAF) 70
Brooke, Gerald 48
Brosnan, Pierce 104
Brown, Coral 102, 104
Buchan, John 94, 107
Bull, Dr. Gerard 110
Burgess, Guy 16, *28*, 29, 31-2, 102, 104
burst-transmission systems 43, *45*, 64
Burt, Richard *92*
Burton, Richard 97, *97*
Bush, President George 39

Caine, Michael 100, 101, 104, 113
Cambridge spy ring 29, 31-2; *see also* Blunt; Burgess; Maclean, Donald; Philby
cameras 6, *7*, 9, 55, 56, *70*
Capone, Al 74, *76*
Carrol, Madeleine *106-7*
Casablanca, film 101
Casino Royale, film *114*, *114*
Castro, Fidel 116, *116-7*
China 51, 52, 58
Churchill, Odette 94
"Cicero," German agent 111
Clancy, Tom 94
Climate of Treason, The (Boyle) 29

Clinton, General Sir William 32
CNN television channel 69
Cohen, Morris and Lona *see* Kroger, Peter and Helen
Cold War 9, 20, 37, 39, 50, 52, 54, 62, 64, 69, 92, 100, 125
Columbia 38, 74, *75*
COMINT (communications intelligence) 39, 41
Connery, Sean 112, *112-13*, 113
Conrad, Joseph 94
Cookridge, E. H. 96
Costner, Kevin *125*
counterterrorism 37, 38, 61, 72, 77-9, 81-2, 87, 89
Cramer, German consul, Amsterdam 33
Cruz, Martin 94
Crying Game, The, novel and film 107, *108*
Cuban missile crisis *8*, 55, 59
Cumming, Capt. Sir Mansfield (RN) 115
Czechoslovakia 48, 55, 85

Dalton, Timothy 113, 114
Davydov, Vladimir 45
Day of the Jackal, The, novel and film 104, *104*
de Gaulle, President Charles 22, 104
Deacon, Richard 96
"dead letter boxes" 23, 47, *50*, 64, *65*
decryption 9, 18, 23, 25
Defence of the Realm, film 106
Deighton, Len 94, 100
Dejean, Marie-Claire 21
Dejean, Maurice 20-22, *22*
Dementiev, Alexander 49
Dictionary of Espionage (Dobson and Payne) 27, 46
Dien Bien Phu, battle of 65
Dobson, Christopher 27, 46, 49
Donat, Robert *106-7*
Dr No., novel and film 112, *112*
drug trade 38, 74, *74-5*, 81, 82, 83, 85, 92
  cartels 65, 74, 107, 109, 125
Dunaway, Faye *121*
Durham, Carl T. *46*

East Germany 39-40, 45, 64, 99, 101
  HVA (Hauptverwaltung Aufklärung) 86, 97-100
  MfS (Ministerium für Staatssicherheit) 38
  NATO missions in 70

NVA (National Volks Armee) 34
economic espionage 50-51, 52, 68
Edge of Darkness (TV series) 106
Egypt 123-4
Eisenhower, President D. D. *35*, 48
electronic countermeasures 40, 41, 43, 59
electronic eavesdropping 52, 65, 67-8
  "bugs" 65, *66-7*, 67
ELECTRO-OPINT 39, 41
ELINT (electronic intelligence) 39, 40, 62, 65, 67
Elliott, Denholm 106
encryption 43, 64, 68
Englishman Abroad, An, TV play 102
Enigma machine 18, *42-4*; *see also* ULTRA intelligence
ESM 40, 62
espionage, definitions of 6, 8, 9
explosives *84-7*, 85-7, 89, 92

Fahd, King, of Saudi Arabia 59
Falkland Islands 26, 41, 60, 69, 72
Femme Nikita, La, film 124
Fleming, Ian 94, 109, 110, 112, 113, 114
For Your Eyes Only, film, *111*
Ford, Harrison 109
Foreign Correspondent, fil, *105*
Forsyth, Frederick 94, 104, 123
forward-looking infrared sensor (FLIR) *41*
Fourth Protocol, The, novel and film 104
Fox, Edward 104, *104*
France 70, 94, 104
  French Intelligence 22, 50, 51, 70-71
  military forces 77-9
From Russia with Love, film *112*
Fuchs, E. J. Klaus *11*, 16, 45-6, 47, 48
Fujimori, President Alberto 82, 83, *84*
Funeral in Berlin, film 100, 101
Furie, Sidney J. 101

Gallagher, Father Clarence 34
Gandt, Roland 100

Garbo, Greta *100*
Gee, Ethel "Bunty" *26*, 27
Gehlen, General Reinhard
  101, 102
Germany 38, 94, 99
  reunified 39, 97, 99
  see also East Germany;
    West Germany
Geyer, Hans Joachim 101-2
Givishiani, Dzermen 49
Global Positioning Systems
  (GPS) 56
Gold, Harry 46, *46*, 47
Goldfinger, film *112*
Gottleib, Dr. Sidney 114,
  116-18
Grant, Cary *102*
Greene, Graham 94
Greenglass, David 46, 47, *47*
Greenpeace boat incident
  70-71
Gresko, Alexander 39
Guderian, General Heinz *42*
Guevara, Ernesto "Che" 81
Guibaud, Colonel Louis 22
Guillaume, Gunther 98, 99,
  99
Guinness, Alec 102
Gulf War 41, 52, *53*, 58, 59,
  69, 72
Guzman Reynoso, Abimael
  ("Gonzalo") 82, *83*

Hackman, Gene *125*
Hambleton, Prof. Hugh 27
Harrison, Sir Geoffrey 22
Haugen, Sven Erling 48-9
Helms, Richard 116
Henried, Paul *101*
Homolka, Oscar 101
Hoover, Edgar J. *9*, 47, 77, 111
Houghton, Harry *26*, 27
HUMINT (human
  intelligence) 9, 34, 39, 43
Hunt for Red October, The,
  film 113

Illustrated London News 52
industrial espionage 7-8,
  50-51, 52
information, classification,
  definition and sources of
  10
informers 89-92
Infra-Red Linescan (IRLS) *56*,
  58
Inman, Admiral Bobby Ray
  20, 38
Intelligence 6-9
  means of gathering 52,
    54-6, 58-61, 62, 64-6,
    67-9
  methods of gathering 72,
    74, 77-9, 81-3, 85-7,

89-93
  NATO definitions of 7-8, 34
  types of 34, 36-9
  U.S. DoD definitions of 34,
    36, 37, 40
Inter-American Defense
  Board (IADB) 6, 8, 10,
    36, 37, 40, 45
International Freedom
  Foundation conference
  43-4
International Institute of
  Applied Systems
  Analysis, Vienna 49, 50
interrogation activities 10,
  37, 46
Ipcress File, The, novel and
  film 100, 101
IRA activity *86-7*
Iraq, Iraqi forces *53*, 59, 69,
  72, 74, 110
Islamic fundamentalist states
  65
Israel 22-3, 40, 62, 123, 124-5
  British Embassy in 22-3
  forces of 40, 62
  Mossad 23, 62, 109, 123, 125

Jameson, Donald "Jamie" 10,
  43, 44, 68
Japan 45, 51
Johnson, President Lyndon B.
  49
Johnson, Sgt. Robert Lee
  (U.S. Army) 27, *27*

Kassem, General Abdul
  Karim 116
Keaton, Diane *109*
Khrushchev, Nikita 27, *35*,
  58
Kobaladze, Yuri 50
Korbut, Olga 39
Korean war 48
Kosygin, Alexei 49
Kroger, Peter and Helen 48
Kronberg-Sobolevskaya,
  Larissa 21-2
Krotkov, Yuri 20, 22
Kuwait, Iraqi invasion of 59

Le Carré, John 94, 96, *96*, 97
Leigh, Janet *103*
Lemmon, Jack *120*
Liberty, USS 62, *62*
Libya 74, 87
lie detectors 16, 23
listening devices *7, 68-9, 71*;
  see also electronic
  eavesdropping
Little Drummer Girl, novel
  and film 107, *109*
Living Daylights, The, film,

113-14
Lonsdale, Gordon 13, 26, 27
Lotz, Wolfgang 122, *122-3*,
  124
Lumumba, Patrice 116

Mackenzie, Compton 114
Maclean, Donald 16, *28*, 29,
  31-2
Maclean, Melinda *29*, 31
Man from UNCLE, The, film
  118
Manchurian Candidate, The,
  film *103*
Manhattan Project 46
maritime intelligence 62
Martin, William H. 20, *20*
Masterman, Sir John 111
Mata Hari *4*, 32-3, *33*
Mata Hari, film *100*
McCallum, David *118*
McKenna, Virginia 94
McMahon, Senator Brien *46*
Meir, Golda *123*
microfilm 64, *65*
Mirinenko, E. S. 50
Missing, film *120*
Mitchell, Bernon F. *20*
Montgomery, Field Marshal,
  Viscount 34
Moore, Roger *95, 111*, 112, 113,
  115
Moscow, May Day parade in
  52

NATO 27, 37, 39, 40, 62, 65,
  69
  definitions of information
  6-8, 34, 36
Neagle, Anna 94
Nelan, Bruce W. 51
Newman, Paul *103*
Newsweek 36, 83, 85
Night Manager, The, (Le
  Carré) 96
Ninio, Marcelle *123*
Niven, David 114, *114*
Nixon, President Richard M.
  99
No Way Out, film *125*
Northern Ireland *73*, 79,
  80-81, 85
Norway 48-50
Notorious, film, *102*

Odessa File, novel and film
  123
Odette, film 94
Old Country, The (Bennett)
  102
Olsen, Dr. Frank 116
one-line code pads 43
Orly Airport, Paris 27

Patriot Games, novel and film
  107, *109*
Payne, Ronald 27, 46, 49
Peck, Bob 106, 107
Penkovsky, Colonel Oleg 10,
  12, 13
Peru 38, 74, 82-3, *82-4*, 85
Petrov, G. G. 50
Philby, Harold "Kim" *28*, 29,
  30, 31, *36*, 102
photocopiers 52, 64
photography 6, 9, 27, 43, 45,
  52, 56, 58
Pincher, Chapman 96
Pinochet, President Augusto
  38
Popov, Dusko *110*, 110-11
Popov, General Pyotr 10
"Portland Spy Ring" 26, 27,
  48
Powers, Francis Gary 21,
  57-8, 58-9
Prime, Geoffrey 20, *21*, 23, 25
Private View, A, (Bennett)
  104
Pueblo, USS 62, *63*

Radar 40, *40*, 41, 43-4, 59
radio intercepts 9, 40, 41, 43,
  52, 60
radio transmitters/receivers
  7, 41, 44-5, 64, 116
Rainbow Warrior 70-71
Rains, Claude *101, 102*
Rea, Stephen *108*
Rebet, Lev 119-20
Redford, Robert 121
Reilly, Capt. Sydney 14, *16*,
  114
Remotely Piloted Vehicle
  (RPV) 37, 40, 72
Ritchie, Rhona 22-3
Rodriguez-Gacha, Jose
  Gonzalo 74
Rosenberg, Julius and Ethel
  32, 46, *47*, 47-8, 49
Rothsay, HMS 12
Royal Air Force 41
Royal Navy 10
Russia House, The (Le Carré)
  96

Salem, "Colonel" Emad 87, 89
satellite reconnaissance 6, 9,
  21, 45, 52, *53*, 55-6
satellites 55, 59, 72
Scharansky, Anatoly *92*
Schell, Maximilian 124
Secret Agent, The (Conrad) 94
security classification 17
sexual relations 19-22, 31, 32
Shackley, Theodore 50, 51

Sheehan, Neil 16
Shining Path organization 82, *82-3*, 83
Sideways Looking Airborne Radar (SLAR) *56*, 58
SIGINT (Signals Intelligence) 19, 39, 41
Silberzahn, Claude 50
Sinatra, Frank *103*
Skardon, William 46
Soviet Union 10, 12, 14, 26, 27, 29, 31, 34, 38, 44, 45, 46, 48, 50, 52, *54*, 58, 62, 69, 72, 92
  agents of 65, 67, 81
  forces in Germany 54
  GRU 13, 34, 46
  KGB 12, 13, 16, 20, 22, 23, 25, 26, 27, 43, 36, 38, 45, 48, 49, 50, 68, 86, 98, 114, 118-20
  spy ships of 62, *63*
Space Shuttle 56
Spacek, Sissy 120
spies *see* agents
  motivations of 10, 29, 32, 46, 94
Spindel, Bernard *66*
spoof equipment 44-5
Spy Who Came in from the Cold, The (Le Carré) 96, 97, *97*
Spy Who Loved Me, The, film *115*
Spycatcher (Wright) 14, *14*
Stalin, Josef 38, 114
Stashinsky, Bogdan 119-20
Sun Tzu Wu 6, 9, 32
Szabo, Violette 94

Tearle, Godfrey *106*
TECHINT (Technical Intelligence) 43, 45, 50
terrorism 8, 29, 74, 77, 79, 81-2, *82-91*, 85-7, 89-92, 125
  see also counter-terrorism
Teufelberge, Berlin 39
Thatcher, Margaret 14, 26
Thermal Imaging 60-61, *61*
Thirty-Nine Steps, The, novel and films *106-7*, 107
Thornburgh, Attorney General Dick *74*
Three Days of the Condor, film *121*
Time magazine 50, 51, 96
Torn Curtain, film *103*
Tube Alloys research project 45

ULTRA intelligence 18-19, *42*, 43, 44
Unattended Ground Sensors

(UGS) 61
uncontrolled sources 13-14
United Kingdom 14, 16, 26, 70
  GCCS *42*
  GCHQ 20, 23
  MI5 14, 22, 46
  MI6 114
  National Security Classifications 18-19
  SAS 89-90
  SOE 14
  Soviet diplomats expelled from 39
  Underwater Weapons Establishment 27
United States 16, 17, 23, 70, 83
  CIA 10, 43, 50, 58, 68, 74, 93, 114, 116
    equipment used by 116, 118, 120-21
  Department of Defense 6, 8, 10, 17
    definitions used by 6, 8, 10
    definitions of intelligence 34, 36, 37, 40, 41, 45
    security classifications 17
  and economic intelligence 50-51
  FBI 23, 27, 48, 50, 77, 87, 111
  Joint Congressional Atomic Committee *46*
  Manhattan Project 46
  Moscow embassy of 67, *67*, 69
  National Security Agency (NSA) 20, 68
  Special Forces (Green Berets) *36*
  USAID program, Vietnam 16
United States Air Force 40, *55*, 58, 59, 83
United States Marine Corps *41*, 60
United States Navy 25, 62
unmanned air vehicle (UAV) *37*

Vann, John 16
Vassall, John *18*, 19-20
Vatican 34, 36
Vaughan, Robert *118-19*
Vietnam war *36*, 40-41, 60, 61, 65
Voight, John 124
Voroshilov, M. *22*

Walker, Lt. Cdr. Arthur James (U.S. Navy) 23, *25*

Walker, John Anthony 23, *24*
Walker, Seaman Michael Lance (U.S. Navy) 23, *24*
Walker spy ring 23, *24*, 25, 43
Warsaw Pact 13, 34, 39, 44, 45, 58, 62, 65, 69
West, Nigel 96
West Germany 45, 98, 99, 100
  BfV (Office for Protection of the Constitution) 98, 99
  BND (Bundesnachrichten-dienst) 101
Whittaker, Forrest *108*
Whitworth, Jerry Alfred 23,

23, 25
Wiseman, Sir William 16
Wolf, Lieut. Gen. Markus Johannes 98, *98-9*
Wright, Peter 14, *15*
Wynne, Greville Maynard *13*, 26

Yakovlev, Anatoli 46, 47, 48
Young, Sean *125*

Zeele, Marguerite *see* Mata Hari

ACKNOWLEDGMENTS

The author and publisher would like to thank D23 for designing the book; Stephen Small, the editor; Sara Dunphy and Suzanne O'Farrell for the picture research; Susan Brown and Nicki Giles for production; and the following institutions and agencies for providing the pictures:

Army Information Services, Northern Ireland, pages: 80
Associated Press, pages: 1, 15, 50(top), 63(bottom), 69, 70, 90-1, 122-3
Aviation Photographs International, pages: 2-3, 53(bottom), 56(both), 57(bottom)
The Bettmann Archive, pages: 11, 13, 33(both), 48(both), 49, 65(bottom), 71(bottom), 96
Brompton Books, pages: 14, 53(top), 60(top), 95, 97, 103(top), 106, 108-9(all three), 111, 112(bottom left & right), 113, 115, 118, 119(both), 120, 121, 124, 125
Bundesarchive, pages: 42(bottom), 44(top)
Counter Spy Shop, pages: 64(bottom), 71(top)
John Frost, pages: 19, 21(bottom), 30
GEC-Marconi, pages: 37, 41(both), 45, 61
HQ Northern Ireland, pages: 73
Hulton-Deutsch, pages: 16, 28(bottom left & right), 31, 42(top), 54(bottom), 99
Imperial War Museum, London, pages: 43
Lockheed-California Company, pages: 8(top)
National Film Archive, London, pages: 100, 102, 103(bottom), 105(both), 107, 114
Reuters/Bettmann, pages: 17, 38, 40(top), 50(bottom), 63(top), 75(both), 81, 82, 83, 84(both), 85, 86(both), 87, 88, 89(both), 92, 93, 98
Robert Hunt Library, pages: 7, 44(bottom)
UPI/Bettmann, pages: 6, 9, 12(both), 18, 20, 21(top), 22, 23, 24(both), 25, 26, 27, 28(top), 29, 35, 36(bottom), 39, 40(bottom), 46-7(all four), 48(top), 51, 54(top), 57(top), 58, 62(both), 64(bottom), 65(top), 66(both), 68, 74, 76, 77, 78, 79, 110, 116-17
United Artists, pages: 112(top)
U.S. Air Force, pages: 55, 59
U.S. Army: 36
U.S. Department of Defense, pages: 8(bottom)
U.S. Department of State, pages: 67(both)
U.S. Navy, pages: 32, 60(bottom)
Universal Studios, pages: 104
Warner Bros./Vitagraph inc., pages: 100-1